truly simple

_____

# kristin cavallari

# truly simple

## 140 Healthy Recipes for Weekday Cooking

RODALE
new york

For Camden, Jaxon, and Saylor,
my favorite people to eat with.
I'm most grateful for you three.

# contents

# truly me

*When my publisher asked me if I'd write a book without the help of a chef, my immediate reaction was "No way, I can't do it alone." The help I had for my other cookbooks was always my security blanket. But then I sat on this request for a few weeks and realized I absolutely can, and in fact, I'm up for the challenge. But more, I'm up for letting everyone see the real me. I'm excited at the thought of sharing my weekday meals— the food I make with my kids, nothing fancy, nothing too hard or complicated—with everyone. My* real *life.*

And to be honest, of all the books I've done, I enjoyed the process of making this one the most. Just me, in my kitchen, with my ideas, my experiments, and my inspiration—and all based on my schedule. With the help of my taste testers (which mostly consisted of my kids and a few friends), I found this process the most relaxing, enjoyable, and rewarding. I'm my most comfortable at home in my cozy clothes and without makeup, so being able to create this book while doing just that was honestly a dream come true. For about five months, my days consisted of making yummy food and going to the grocery store, which was a nice departure from the past few years during which I was hustling—filming a TV show, going to my office at Uncommon James, and hosting different gigs among other things. It felt like I was able to take a little break from life. Just be Mom and be in my kitchen. I loved every second.

The inspiration for these recipes came from all over—some I've had for years, others came from different restaurants where I've eaten, still others came from images I've seen on Instagram or in magazines. And some were just special requests from my kiddos. And obviously, keeping the theme in mind, all the recipes had to be effortless. Don't get me wrong, there's a time and a place for elaborate meals, which I do really enjoy making when the time is right, but this cookbook is all about those busy weekdays, running from one thing to the next while still wanting a delicious, healthy meal on the table for the fam.

The theme of this book mirrors my life during the past few years: I'm not trying to be something I'm not, and I'm okay with letting everyone see the real me. I've stepped into my comfort zone, and it feels really damn good. I've let go of perfectionism and trying to do it all. In a general sense, I'm more at peace. And it shows through my cooking. I'm all about simplicity these days.

That's not to say the foundation of how I eat has changed, but I've definitely swayed in a few areas. And that's okay. Health and our own personal journey are forever evolving, and hopefully, we are continually growing and coming to a better understanding of ourself.

My philosophy has always been to eat real food and to limit processed stuff. However, the thing I've bent the most is my old rule: "Don't eat anything white." I've come to believe that, even if something is white (flour, sugar, salt), as long as it's in its natural state, then you can have at it. Maybe white sugar isn't the worst thing for us on the planet. And even if it is, having a little bit here and there helps me stay sane in this crazy world. Life is too short to always say no to something so sweet.

> I'm not trying to be something I'm not, and I'm okay with letting everyone see the real me.

So, if you take away just one thing from this book, let it be this: Let's not be so hard on ourselves and instead let's enjoy life because it goes too damn fast. Hopefully, you actually do love these recipes and take away much, much more than just that one thought. But you get what I'm saying.

pantry

Eating real, whole food is a philosophy I've lived by for more than ten years. Being as close to its natural state as possible is how I believe food was intended. It's what makes our bodies function at their highest potential. Over the years, what I allow in my kitchen has changed slightly (for example, two years ago you never would have found raw cane sugar in my pantry, but now you will), but the ethos is the same: Eat processed food as minimally as possible to live a healthy life. The following are the staples I always have in my house, the items I use regularly to feel my best, and the things I need to make cooking fun and delicious.

## equipment

Vitamix blender

Food processor

Mandoline

Microplane zester

Nut milk bag—can be ordered on Amazon if your local grocery store doesn't carry them

Crock-Pot

## on the counter

Tons of fresh fruit and vegetables, such as avocados, bananas, oranges, tomatoes, as well as acorn squash, butternut squash, garlic, shallots, and sweet potatoes

## in the freezer

More berries

More veggies, including cauliflower florets and spinach

Bananas (I wait until they're really ripe, then I peel and freeze them in a zip-top bag.)

## in the fridge

Wild-caught fish, such as cod, salmon, and sea bass

Grass-fed beef and bison

Pasture-raised organic chicken

Organic, pasture-raised eggs (I have a chicken coop, so sometimes you'll find these on my counter as well, since homegrown eggs don't have to be put in the fridge for a couple weeks.)

**Fruit and veggies:** berries, broccoli, carrots, cauliflower, cucumbers, grapefruits, green beans, lemons, lettuce, limes, spinach, and zucchini

**Raw nut butters:** almond, cashew, macadamia, and walnut

**Goat's- and sheep's-milk cheeses,** such as raw goat cheddar, Manchego, and Drunken Goat

**Sheep's-milk yogurt**

**Mayo** (I like the ones made with avocado oil, such as Primal Kitchen)

**Butter** (both goat's-milk butter and organic, pasture-raised butter)

**Fresh herbs:** basil, cilantro, parsley, rosemary, and thyme

**Condiments:** coconut aminos, Dijon mustard, hot sauce, ketchup, and pure maple syrup

**Nondairy milks:** almond and oat

**White miso paste**

**Pickles**

**Dates**

## in the pantry

**Nuts:** almonds, cashews, pecans, pine nuts, pistachios, and walnuts

**Pasta:** brown rice pasta, buckwheat soba noodles, and lentil pasta

**Oils:** avocado oil, extra-virgin olive oil, toasted sesame oil, virgin coconut oil

**Salts:** pure Italian fine sea salt and Icelandic flake salt

**Dried herbs and spices:** black pepper, cumin, garlic powder, onion powder, red pepper flakes, and smoked paprika

**Sweeteners:** coconut sugar, Manuka honey, powdered sugar, raw cane sugar, and raw honey

**Flours:** almond flour, arrowroot powder, cassava flour, coconut flour, and oat flour

**Full-fat coconut milk**

**Tamari**

**Chicken stock**

**Anchovies**

# drinks

# whipped coffee

Whipped coffee started trending at the height of the pandemic, when everyone was at home trying out new culinary treats. It instantly caught my eye because of how elaborate the presentation is and how comforting it looked. This is a treat that I like making on the weekends when I have some extra time in the morning. Just make sure the water is boiling hot when you add it, otherwise the coffee won't get super thick and frothy.

---

*Serves 1*

—

2 tablespoons instant coffee (I like the brand Four Sigmatic)

1 tablespoon raw cane sugar or raw honey

1 cup Brazil Nut Milk (page 261)

Ground cinnamon (optional), for garnish

1. Place the instant coffee, sugar, and 2 tablespoons boiling water in the bowl of a stand mixer. Turn the mixer on low for a few seconds, then increase the speed to high for 3 to 4 minutes, until the mixture is whipped and fluffy. I like to place a dish towel over my stand mixer so I don't make a mess.

2. Pour the Brazil Nut Milk in a tall glass or mason jar. Spoon the whipped coffee on top. Top with ground cinnamon, if desired. Enjoy right away.

# coffee spritzer

There's a little coffee shop near my house that's one of those "tiny houses" (it was actually featured on the DIY Network's *Tiny House, Big Living*), and they serve these coffee spritzers. It basically tastes like a coffee-flavored soda. You can make up any flavor combination you like. I personally use hazelnut and vanilla extract. Feel free to leave out all flavoring, if you prefer, and just do the base—it's still good.

*Serves 1*

—

¾ cup iced coffee or cold-brewed coffee

¾ cup sparkling water

½ teaspoon pure maple syrup

½ teaspoon pure hazelnut extract (optional)

½ teaspoon pure vanilla extract (optional)

2 tablespoons full-fat coconut milk

Pour the coffee, sparkling water, maple syrup, and, if using, the hazelnut and vanilla extracts into a large glass. Stir to combine. Add a handful of ice, top with the coconut milk, and serve.

# caffè salentino

This recipe is inspired by my roots in the south of Italy. Italians like their espresso iced with a hint of almond milk. I've swapped the almond milk for coconut milk and added a little almond extract, because coconut milk is thicker and gives this coffee drink a touch more creaminess.

---

*Serves 1*

—

1 to 2 shots espresso

½ teaspoon pure almond extract

1 teaspoon pure maple syrup

1 tablespoon full-fat coconut milk

Mix the espresso, almond extract, and maple syrup together in a mug or cup. Place ice in a small glass, pour the espresso mixture on top, add the coconut milk, and serve.

# london fog

A few times a year I like to prove to myself that I can go without coffee, so I'll take a break from drinking it daily. My logic behind this is, I don't want to be dependent on anything . . . so taking breaks validates that I don't *need* coffee. During these breaks, I'll make these London Fogs. They're comforting, just like coffee is in the morning, and are a nice departure for me from the normal latte route.

---

*Serves 2*

—

2 Earl Grey tea bags

1 cup full-fat coconut milk

1 scoop your favorite collagen powder

½ teaspoon pure vanilla extract

1 teaspoon raw honey

1. Place 12 ounces hot water in a medium bowl. Add the tea bags and steep for 5 minutes. Remove and discard the tea bags.

2. Meanwhile, in a small saucepan, warm the coconut milk over medium heat until it is hot but not boiling. Whisk in the collagen powder, vanilla, and honey. Add the tea and stir to combine.

3. Pour into 2 mugs and enjoy.

# peppermint collagen matcha latte

I can't drink coffee past noon because I'll never fall asleep (yes, I'm very sensitive to it), so matcha is my go-to. It's my favorite afternoon pick-me-up that doesn't keep me up all night. I like jazzing up my matchas, so here I've added peppermint for taste as well as chlorella for its vitamins, minerals, and antioxidants. I've also included collagen powder because it's great for joints, skin, hair, and nails, but that's optional for my vegans.

---

*Serves 1*

—

1¼ cups full-fat coconut milk

½ teaspoon pure peppermint extract

1½ teaspoons matcha powder

1½ teaspoons raw honey

¼ teaspoon chlorella powder

1 scoop your favorite collagen powder (optional)

1. In a small saucepan, combine the coconut milk, peppermint extract, matcha, honey, chlorella, and collagen powder, if using, and warm the mixture over medium heat. Whisk until fully combined and to your desired temperature.

2. Pour into a mug and enjoy.

# chocolate cherry smoothie

Chocolate and cherry is a classic flavor combo. It's rich and luxurious, and this smoothie is just that. Frozen avocado makes smoothies super creamy, and the handful of spinach here gives you extra nutrients (plus, you can't taste it at all). I make this when I want something chocolaty and decadent. For the frozen avocado, peel and pit the avocado, then place it in a zip-top bag and freeze it overnight. I always have a stash on hand in the freezer for smoothies.

---

*Serves 1*

—

1½ cups almond milk

1 tablespoon raw cacao powder

2 dates, pitted and coarsely chopped

½ avocado, frozen

½ cup frozen spinach

1 tablespoon hemp seeds

½ cup frozen dark cherries

1. Place the almond milk, cacao powder, dates, avocado, spinach, hemp seeds, and cherries in a high-powered blender. Blend on high until smooth, about 30 seconds.

2. Pour in a glass and enjoy right away.

# sweet green smoothie

I'm one of those people who really enjoys green juice, even if it's just pure greens without an apple or other sweet fruit. But the only way to get my kids to drink a green smoothie is to add fruit or some other sweetness. I love this smoothie because it's not overly sweet, but it's still packed with a ton of greens, and my kids will actually drink it. When I make this for my kiddos, I double the recipe, then split it among the three of them, since one full serving is usually a little too much for them.

---

*Serves 1*

—

1 tablespoon chia seeds

¾ cup coconut water

½ medium English cucumber, peeled and coarsely chopped

½ cup packed spinach

½ avocado, frozen

1 small green apple, cored and coarsely chopped

Juice of 1 lime (about 2 tablespoons)

½ cup almond milk or Brazil Nut Milk (page 261)

1. Place the chia seeds, coconut water, cucumber, spinach, avocado, green apple, lime juice, and nut milk in a high-powered blender. Blend on high until smooth, about 30 seconds.

2. Pour in a glass and enjoy right away.

berry protein
smoothie, page 30

sweet green
smoothie, page 27

chocolate cherry
smoothie, page 26

# berry protein smoothie

This smoothie is perfect for breakfast because it's really filling—with yogurt, a whole zucchini, berries, and a ton of protein, with the nut butter, chia seeds, and hemp seeds. Zucchini is great to throw in smoothies because you can't taste it and it's an easy way to get some extra greens in. During the summer months, I typically have a smoothie every single morning. I could honestly live on them, since they're refreshing and an easy way to get so many nutrients in (they're also a breeze to whip up!). So this particular smoothie is made a few times per week.

---

*Serves 1*

—

1 tablespoon nut butter, such as almond or cashew

1 teaspoon chia seeds

1 teaspoon hemp seeds

1 scoop your favorite collagen powder

1 small zucchini, coarsely chopped

½ cup frozen blueberries

1 cup almond milk

2 teaspoons raw honey

¼ cup plain yogurt

1. Place the nut butter, chia seeds, hemp seeds, collagen powder, zucchini, blueberries, almond milk, honey, and yogurt in a high-powered blender. Blend on high until smooth, about 30 seconds.

2. Pour in a glass and enjoy right away.

# island girl juice

This juice is a powerhouse of health benefits and is incredibly refreshing, perfect for a warm summer day (I like making this when it's warm outside—sipping it in the sun while pretending to be on an exotic island!). Cilantro is great for helping the body rid itself of toxins such as heavy metals (thank you to the Medical Medium for teaching me that), so I try to incorporate it whenever I can. Ginger fights infections in the body and boosts digestion. Pineapple and green apple balance this juice out, giving it the perfect amount of sweetness.

---

*Serves 1*

—

½ cup chopped fresh pineapple

1 medium green apple, cored and coarsely chopped

1 medium English cucumber, peeled and coarsely chopped

Juice of 1 lime (about 2 tablespoons)

1-inch piece fresh ginger, peeled and coarsely chopped

¼ cup chopped fresh cilantro

1. Place the pineapple, green apple, cucumber, lime juice, ginger, and cilantro in a high-powered blender with ¼ cup filtered water. Blend on high until smooth, about 30 seconds.

2. Pour over ice in a glass and enjoy right away.

# honey maple lemonade

My kids love lemonade during the warmer months, but store-bought brands are usually full of additives, so I make my own version at home. I like to sweeten it with honey and maple syrup for the vitamins and minerals. Plus, my kids enjoy helping me make this—and whenever they want to be in the kitchen with me, that's always a win.

*Makes about 4 cups*

—

½ cup fresh lemon juice (from about 3 large lemons)

¼ cup raw honey

2 tablespoons pure maple syrup

4 cups filtered water

1. Place the lemon juice, honey, and maple syrup in a pitcher. Whisk to combine. Add the water and stir to combine. Pour over ice in a glass to enjoy right away or place in the fridge to chill for an hour before drinking.

2. The lemonade will keep well in the fridge for up to 7 days.

# breakfast

# blueberry cinnamon sugar-baked oats

Oatmeal is eaten at least three times a week at my house, since my kids and I all love it, so I'm always trying new ways to switch it up. The combination of blueberry, cinnamon, and sugar will forever be a favorite of mine when it comes to baked goods, so I thought, "Why not try it with oatmeal?!" Success. This oatmeal is baked to make it extra luxurious and comforting.

---

*Serves 6*

—

2 tablespoons virgin coconut oil, melted, plus more for the pan

2 large eggs

¼ cup pure maple syrup

¼ teaspoon salt

2½ teaspoons ground cinnamon, divided

½ cup coconut sugar

1½ teaspoons pure vanilla extract

¼ teaspoon ground nutmeg

1 (13.5 oz.) can full-fat coconut milk

1 pint blueberries

2 cups gluten-free rolled oats

1. Preheat the oven to 350°F. Grease an 8 × 8-inch baking dish with coconut oil.

2. In a large bowl, whisk together the eggs, maple syrup, coconut oil, salt, 1½ teaspoons of the cinnamon, ¼ cup of the coconut sugar, the vanilla, nutmeg, and coconut milk until combined. Stir in the blueberries and oats.

3. Transfer the mixture to the prepared baking dish. Sprinkle with the remaining 1 teaspoon cinnamon and ¼ cup coconut sugar.

4. Bake for 30 to 35 minutes, until golden brown and bubbling. Let cool 10 minutes before serving.

# yogurt parfaits
## with grain-free granola and warm berry sauce

I'll never get sick of yogurt parfaits. Or granola. They're two staples in my house. Actually, this recipe has three of my staples, if you include the Warm Berry Sauce (page 257). The granola is also yummy as a snack by itself and the Warm Berry Sauce is good on just about anything—crepes, ice cream, oatmeal, you name it. If you don't want dairy in this recipe, then swap the plain yogurt for plain coconut-milk yogurt.

*Serves 2*

—

**grain-free granola**

½ cup flaxseeds

1 cup pumpkin seeds

1 cup walnuts

2 cups almonds

½ cup hemp seeds

¼ cup virgin coconut oil, melted

½ cup pure maple syrup

1 tablespoon pure vanilla extract

1 teaspoon ground cinnamon

½ teaspoon ground nutmeg

½ teaspoon salt

½ cup unsweetened, shredded coconut

2 cups plain yogurt

½ cup Warm Berry Sauce (page 257)

Pure maple syrup (optional), for drizzling

1. Preheat the oven to 325°F. Line a large baking sheet with parchment paper.

2. Place the flaxseeds, pumpkin seeds, walnuts, almonds, and hemp seeds in a food processor and pulse a few times until combined and the nuts are broken up. Pulse in the coconut oil, maple syrup, vanilla, cinnamon, nutmeg, and salt until combined. It should be a chunky doughlike consistency.

3. Spread out the granola mixture on the prepared baking sheet. Bake for 20 to 25 minutes, until golden brown. Remove the baking sheet from the oven and top the granola mixture with the coconut. Let cool, then break into chunks (about 5 cups total). The granola will keep well in an airtight container on the counter for up to 14 days.

4. Place ½ cup of the yogurt in the bottom of each of 2 mason jars or tall glasses. Add to each ¼ cup of the berry sauce, then another ½ cup of the yogurt. Top each with ½ cup of the granola. Drizzle with a little maple syrup, if desired. Enjoy right away.

# gluten-free honey biscuits

Everyone in my house loves carbs. *Loves*. My kids go nuts for these
biscuits, which are a touch sweet and incredibly comforting. They
gobble them up for breakfast but also devour them as a snack. Maybe
it's because I'm a die-hard carb girl, but these biscuits—warm and with
a little butter on top—make me think this is what heaven must be like.
I make these gluten-free because that's how we eat on a regular basis.
Honestly, I find we all just feel better when we eat gluten-free the
majority of the time.

---

*Makes 12*

—

2½ cups almond flour

¾ cup arrowroot powder

½ teaspoon baking soda

½ teaspoon salt

¼ cup (½ stick) cold, unsalted
butter, cut into small cubes,
plus more, melted, for serving

¼ cup raw honey

2 large eggs

1. Preheat the oven to 350°F. Line a large baking sheet with
parchment paper.

2. In a large bowl, whisk together the flour, arrowroot powder,
baking soda, and salt until combined. Using your hands, cut in
the butter until it resembles sand or coarse crumbs.

3. In a small bowl, whisk together the honey and eggs. Add the
egg mixture to the flour mixture and stir until a soft dough
forms, being careful not to overmix.

4. Spoon the batter onto the baking sheet, about ¼ cup per
biscuit. Bake for 15 to 18 minutes, until golden brown. Let
cool for 5 minutes.

5. Serve the biscuits warm brushed with melted butter.
The biscuits will keep well in an airtight container on the
counter for up to 7 days.

# honey ricotta pancakes

My kids will always eat pancakes, and I like how relatively easy these are to whip up in the morning. I love ricotta in just about anything (it must be my Italian roots), including these pancakes. The ricotta balances perfectly with the touch of honey. Fluffy and flavorful, these pancakes make for a healthy yet indulgent breakfast.

*Serves 4*

—

2 large eggs, separated

1½ cups oat flour

1½ teaspoons baking powder

½ teaspoon salt

1½ cups almond milk

1 cup whole-milk ricotta

1 tablespoon raw honey

1 teaspoon pure vanilla extract

Virgin coconut oil, for the pan

Maple syrup (optional), for serving

Powdered sugar (optional), for serving

Warm Berry Sauce (page 257; optional), for serving

1. Place the egg whites in the bowl of a stand mixer, then beat on high until they form stiff peaks, 2 to 3 minutes.

2. In a large bowl, combine the flour, baking powder, and salt.

3. In another large bowl, whisk together the almond milk, egg yolks, ricotta, honey, and vanilla. Fold in the egg whites. Add the wet ingredients to the dry ingredients and mix them together.

4. Warm the coconut oil in a skillet over medium heat. Spoon the batter, using about ¼ cup per pancake, onto the skillet and cook for 2 to 3 minutes, until the pancakes start to bubble. Flip them over and cook for 3 minutes on the other side. Repeat to make more pancakes with the remaining batter, adding oil to the skillet as needed.

5. Top the pancakes with maple syrup, powdered sugar, berry sauce, or your favorite toppings and serve.

# veggie, bacon, and feta crustless quiche

This quiche is very easy to make—you can essentially throw anything in and it will still taste good. However, for the sake of this recipe, I've included my current favorite combo: veggies, for the health boost, plus bacon and feta. Yum. I actually love a regular quiche, but for the ease of this recipe I've made this one crustless. And the flavor is so good you won't miss it.

---

*Serves 6*

—

Coconut oil, for the pan

1 (12-ounce) package bacon

½ cup finely chopped shallots

3 cups chopped spinach

6 large eggs

1 cup full-fat coconut milk

¾ cup crumbled feta cheese

Salt and freshly ground black pepper

½ cup halved cherry tomatoes

¼ cup packed fresh basil leaves

1. Preheat the oven to 350°F. Grease a pie dish with coconut oil.

2. In a large skillet, cook the bacon over medium-high heat until just before it crisps up, about 4 minutes on each side. Transfer the bacon to a paper towel–lined plate. Once cool, chop the bacon, then set it aside.

3. Add the shallots to the same skillet with the bacon fat. Sauté the shallots over medium heat until slightly caramelized and golden brown, about 5 minutes. Add the spinach and sauté until wilted, about 1 minute. Remove the skillet from the heat.

4. In a large bowl, whisk together the eggs, coconut milk, and feta, adding a big pinch each of salt and pepper. Stir in the tomatoes. Pour the egg mixture into the prepared pie dish and place the basil leaves on top.

5. Bake, uncovered, for 45 minutes, or until the center is set. Let cool for 20 minutes before serving.

6. The quiche will keep well in the fridge for up to 5 days.

# crepes
## with honey lemon drizzle

My kids would say this is their favorite recipe in the entire book. When I first started making these crepes, my boys ate so many that for months I was making them twice a day (yes, eventually I just started to double the recipe). The beauty of these is that you can literally put anything you want in them. We do either scrambled eggs with bacon and hot sauce or go the sweet route with Warm Berry Sauce (page 257), the Honey Lemon Drizzle I use here, whipped cream, chocolate sauce, or even just a sweetened nut butter. The sky is the limit! If you're making savory crepes instead of sweet, just leave the vanilla out.

---

*Makes 4 large crepes*

—

4 large eggs

1 tablespoon coconut flour

2 teaspoons virgin coconut oil, melted, plus more for the pan

1 teaspoon pure vanilla extract (if making sweet crepes)

Salt

½ cup arrowroot powder

Nut butter, such as almond or cashew, for serving

Warm Berry Sauce (page 257; optional), for serving

Honey Lemon Drizzle (recipe follows; optional), for serving

1. In a medium bowl, whisk together the eggs, coconut flour, coconut oil, vanilla, 2 tablespoons water, and a pinch of salt until well combined. Add the arrowroot powder and whisk until smooth.

2. Warm a 10-inch skillet over medium heat. Lightly grease with coconut oil.

3. Once the pan is hot, pour about ¼ cup batter on the skillet and immediately swirl it around on the pan so it's covering the whole pan in a thin, even layer. Cook for 45 seconds, until it's not liquid-y anymore, then flip and cook an additional 30 to 45 seconds. Repeat to make more crepes with the remaining batter, adding oil to the skillet as needed.

4. Fill the crepes with the nut butter, berry sauce, and lemon drizzle, if desired, or your favorite ingredients. We fill our crepes, then roll them up, but you could also fold the crepes, then top them with your ingredients.

# honey lemon drizzle

¼ cup fresh lemon juice (from about 2 lemons)

1 teaspoon lemon zest

½ cup raw honey

1 tablespoon arrowroot powder

*This drizzle is good warm or cold. When cool, it transforms into a jam-like consistency.*

1. In a small saucepan over medium-high heat, whisk together the lemon juice, lemon zest, honey, and arrowroot powder. Bring to a boil, then simmer, whisking occasionally, until thickened, 2 to 4 minutes.

2. Stored in a mason jar or other airtight container, this drizzle will keep well in the fridge for up to 10 days.

# egg bowl

I had been throwing this bowl together for years when I finally made it for some friends who were staying with me and one of them asked for the recipe. I didn't realize it needed an actual recipe . . . but here ya go! This bowl is my go-to when I'm being healthy but want something easy and filling in the morning.

---

*Serves 1*

—

2 large eggs

1 tablespoon full-fat coconut milk

Virgin coconut oil, for the pan

1½ teaspoons extra-virgin olive oil, plus more for drizzling

1 cup packed greens, such as spinach or arugula, chopped

Salt

2 tablespoons soft goat's-milk cheese

½ avocado, sliced

Flaky sea salt

Red pepper flakes

1. In a small bowl, whisk together the eggs and coconut milk.

2. Warm a little coconut oil in a medium skillet over medium heat. Add the egg mixture and scramble until cooked through, 3 to 4 minutes. Place in a bowl and cover to keep warm.

3. In another medium skillet, warm the olive oil over medium heat. Add the spinach and a pinch of salt. Sauté for 2 minutes, until wilted. Add the greens to the same bowl as the eggs.

4. Top the eggs and greens with the goat's-milk cheese and avocado. Sprinkle with flaky sea salt and red pepper flakes and drizzle with olive oil. Eat right away.

# poached egg bowls
## with hollandaise sauce

Let's be honest, the best part about eggs Benedict is the hollandaise sauce. This poached egg bowl satisfies my hollandaise craving without weighing me down. I added spinach to get some greens in first thing.

*Serves 2*

—

**hollandaise sauce**

½ cup (1 stick) unsalted butter

3 egg yolks

1 tablespoon fresh lemon juice

1 teaspoon Dijon mustard

¼ teaspoon salt

Cayenne pepper

—

**bowls**

1 teaspoon extra-virgin olive oil

1 cup coarsely chopped spinach

Salt and freshly ground black pepper

4 large eggs

1 tablespoon white wine vinegar

1. Make the hollandaise sauce: In a small saucepan over medium-high heat, melt the butter, then remove the saucepan from the heat.

2. Place the egg yolks, lemon juice, mustard, salt, and a pinch of cayenne pepper in a high-powered blender. Blend until combined, just a few seconds. While the blade is running on medium-low, slowly add the hot butter until it's emulsified (the mixture will thicken slightly and be combined, about 20 seconds). Pour the hollandaise sauce into a small bowl, cover, and set aside.

3. Make the bowls: Warm the olive oil in a skillet over medium heat. Sauté the spinach with a pinch of salt and pepper until wilted, 2 to 3 minutes.

4. To poach the eggs: Crack the eggs in 4 separate ramekins or small bowls. In a medium pot over medium-high heat, simmer enough water so the eggs will be fully submerged. Add a pinch of salt and the white wine vinegar. Using a spoon, start a stirring motion, or a whirlpool, in the water. Gently pour the eggs, one at a time, into the center of the pot. Let poach for 3 to 5 minutes. To remove, use a slotted spoon and place each egg on a paper towel.

5. To serve, divide the spinach between 2 bowls. Place 2 eggs in each bowl and drizzle with the hollandaise sauce.

# loaded breakfast burritos

There's truly nothing better than a good, old-fashioned breakfast burrito. I think less is more when it comes to burritos, so for me, it's all about the eggs followed by the salty crunch of bacon and the creaminess of sour cream and avocado . . . Why add anything else?! These are hearty and filling, so I typically make them on the weekends when I won't be working out shortly after I eat (there's nothing worse than working out on a full stomach!). And yes, I work out only on the weekdays . . . my weekends are to relax!

---

*Serves 2*

—

4 large eggs

Salt

Virgin coconut oil, for the pan

4 slices bacon

1 avocado

¼ teaspoon fresh lime juice

2 tortillas (I like the Siete brand almond flour)

¼ cup sour cream

Hot sauce (optional)

1. In a small bowl, beat the eggs, then add a pinch of salt.

2. Warm a large skillet over medium heat, then coat it with coconut oil. Pour in the eggs and scramble until they're cooked through, about 5 minutes.

3. In another large skillet, cook the bacon over medium-high heat until slightly crispy or as desired. Transfer the cooked bacon to a paper towel–lined plate. Let cool for a couple minutes, then roughly chop.

4. In a small bowl, combine the avocado, lime juice, and a big pinch of salt. Mash with a fork until combined. Set aside.

5. In a large skillet, warm the tortillas over medium heat for about 30 seconds, then remove the skillet from the heat.

6. To build the burritos: Place half of the eggs on a tortilla, followed by half of the avocado mixture, half of the bacon, 2 tablespoons of the sour cream, and hot sauce, if using. Roll it up. Repeat with the remaining ingredients to make the second burrito.

7. Enjoy right away.

# sourdough french toast

When prepared traditionally, sourdough bread is fermented, making it almost gluten-free and tolerable for people with gluten sensitivities. It is hands down my whole family's favorite type of bread. We also love French toast, so I figured, let's combine the two. Just make sure to slice the sourdough bread as thin as possible, otherwise it will be chewy.

---

*Serves 6 to 8*

—

1 (13.5-ounce) can full-fat coconut milk

4 large eggs

2 teaspoons ground cinnamon

½ teaspoon ground nutmeg

1½ teaspoons pure vanilla extract

½ cup pure maple syrup

Salt

1 tablespoon unsalted butter or more as needed

1 loaf sourdough, ends discarded, then cut into ⅛-inch-thick slices

—

**to serve**

Unsalted butter (optional)

Pure maple syrup (optional)

Powdered sugar (optional)

1. In a large bowl, whisk together the coconut milk, eggs, cinnamon, nutmeg, vanilla, maple syrup, and a pinch of salt until smooth.

2. Warm a large skillet over medium-high heat and lightly coat with butter. Dip each slice of bread into the egg mixture, making sure to coat both sides. Add the bread to the skillet and cook until the bread is golden brown, 2 to 3 minutes per side. You'll have to work in batches until all the bread is gone.

3. To serve, place the French toast on a plate and add butter, maple syrup, powdered sugar, or your favorite toppings.

# lemon poppy seed muffins

My older son is my lemon guy, so I created these with him in mind. Truth be told, I love lemon as well. I always say I'm going to make these for Cam but then I end up eating just as many as he does. The lemon in these muffins is not overpowering—it's just a perfect lemon kiss.

---

*Makes 24*

—

2¼ cups oat flour

½ cup almond flour

2 tablespoons poppy seeds

½ teaspoon baking powder

1 teaspoon baking soda

¼ teaspoon salt

¾ cup nut milk, such as Brazil Nut Milk (page 261)

1 teaspoon pure vanilla extract

¼ cup fresh lemon juice (from about 2 lemons)

1 tablespoon lemon zest

2 large eggs

¾ cup pure maple syrup

3 tablespoons virgin coconut oil, melted

1. Preheat the oven to 350°F. Prepare a muffin tin with liners.

2. In a large bowl, stir together the oat flour, almond flour, poppy seeds, baking powder, baking soda, and salt until combined.

3. In another large bowl, whisk together the nut milk, vanilla, lemon juice, lemon zest, eggs, maple syrup, and coconut oil until smooth. Pour the wet mixture into the dry mixture and fold until just combined.

4. Pour the batter into the prepared tin, filling each cup until about two-thirds full. Bake for 20 to 22 minutes, or until a toothpick comes out clean. Let cool 10 minutes before enjoying. The muffins will keep well in an airtight container on the counter for up to 5 days, or in the fridge for up to 7 days.

# tomato and corn
# breakfast tostadas
## with fried eggs

If you like Mexican food, you'll love these. A crispy tostada with runny eggs and all of the traditional flavors, these will make you feel like you just woke up on the beach in Cabo.

---

*Serves 4*

—

3 cups halved cherry tomatoes

1½ cups canned (and drained) or fresh corn

1 medium yellow onion, thinly sliced

2 tablespoons plus ¾ cup avocado oil, plus more for the pan

3 cloves garlic, minced

2 teaspoons minced canned chipotle chiles in adobo sauce

1 teaspoon ground cumin

Salt and freshly ground black pepper

8 tortillas (I like the Siete brand almond flour)

8 large eggs

1 cup refried beans, warmed

2 ounces goat's-milk cheese

3 tablespoons chopped fresh cilantro

1. Preheat the oven to 500°F. Line a large baking sheet with foil.

2. In a large bowl, toss together the tomatoes, corn, onion, 2 tablespoons of the avocado oil, the garlic, chiles, cumin, ½ teaspoon salt, and ¼ teaspoon pepper until combined. Spread the mixture out on the prepared baking sheet. Roast until the tomatoes are just beginning to blister, 12 to 15 minutes.

3. Meanwhile, heat the remaining ¾ cup avocado oil in a large skillet over medium-high heat. Line a second large baking sheet with paper towels.

4. Working with one tortilla at a time, fry in the hot oil, using tongs to make sure it stays submerged. Fry for about 45 seconds, until crisp and golden brown. Transfer to the paper towels. Repeat with the remaining tortillas.

5. Lightly grease another large skillet with avocado oil and set over medium heat. Fry the eggs, working in batches, until cooked as desired. Remove the skillet from the heat.

6. To serve, spread 2 tablespoons refried beans over a tostada. Top with the veggie mixture and 1 egg. Sprinkle with the goat's-milk cheese and cilantro. Repeat with the remaining ingredients. Enjoy right away.

# pesto egg casserole

I've included pesto in recipes throughout this book and I knew I had to figure out a way to get it into the breakfast chapter as well. I grew up eating pesto on eggs, so this recipe was a no-brainer for me. I love this when I have a house full of people and need something easy to make that feeds many.

*Serves 8*

—

¾ cup virgin coconut oil, plus more for the pan

2 cloves garlic, minced

2 large yellow squash, chopped

1 red bell pepper, thinly sliced

1 small yellow onion, thinly sliced

Salt and freshly ground black pepper

6 large eggs

1 cup chopped cherry tomatoes

½ cup Pesto (page 254)

1. Preheat the oven to 350°F. Grease a 9 × 11-inch baking dish with coconut oil.

2. In a large saucepan, warm the coconut oil over medium heat. Add the garlic and cook until fragrant, 1 minute. Add the squash, bell pepper, onion, and a big pinch of salt. Sauté until slightly tender, 5 minutes. Remove the saucepan from the heat.

3. In a large bowl, beat the eggs until combined and slightly fluffy. Add the cooked veggies, tomatoes, and pesto, and stir to combine. Season with salt and pepper.

4. Pour the egg mixture into the prepared baking dish. Bake for 45 to 48 minutes, until the center is set. Let cool for 15 minutes before serving.

# turmeric fried eggs
## with crispy kale

This is a great breakfast when you want to be healthy but still want all the flavor. Kale, which is packed with vitamins and minerals, and turmeric, which helps fight inflammation, will provide a nice start to your day. The chili oil gives these eggs the perfect kick, but if you don't like spicy stuff, then just leave it out.

*Serves 2 to 4*

—

1 bunch Lacinato kale, ribs and stems removed, then chopped

5 tablespoons extra-virgin olive oil

Salt

4 large eggs

1 teaspoon ground turmeric

Chili Oil (page 253; optional)

1. Preheat the oven to 375°F. Line a medium baking sheet with parchment paper.

2. In a large bowl, mix the kale, 2 tablespoons of the olive oil, and a big pinch of salt. Using your hands, massage the kale until it is coated and slightly wilted, 20 to 30 seconds. Place the kale on the prepared baking sheet and bake for 5 to 7 minutes, until it is lightly browned on the edges. Remove the baking sheet from the oven.

3. Meanwhile, fry the eggs: In a large skillet, warm the remaining 3 tablespoons olive oil over medium-high heat. Add the eggs, cook them for 3 minutes, then flip and cook them an additional 2 to 3 minutes. Turn the heat to low and add the turmeric. Tilt the skillet to baste the eggs with the turmeric-oil mixture. Flip the eggs to coat both sides.

4. To serve, place 1 or 2 fried eggs on each plate along with the crispy kale. Drizzle with Chili Oil, if desired, and serve immediately.

# cauliflower oatmeal

It may sound silly to a lot of you, but this is one of my favorite recipes in the whole book. For me, there's something so comforting about oatmeal. And the fact that this oatmeal is made from a vegetable, and it still tastes just as good, makes my heart sing. I load on the toppings to make this a really indulgent bowl. Feel free to swap out any of my topping suggestions for your personal faves.

---

*Serves 1*

—

1 cup Cauliflower Rice (page 260)

½ cup full-fat coconut milk

¼ teaspoon ground cinnamon

½ teaspoon pure vanilla extract

¾ teaspoon pure maple syrup, plus more (optional) for topping

1 teaspoon chia seeds

2 large strawberries, sliced (optional)

1 tablespoon unsweetened, shredded coconut (optional)

1 tablespoon hemp seeds (optional)

1 tablespoon bee pollen (optional)

1 tablespoon cacao nibs (optional)

1½ tablespoons nut butter, such as almond or walnut (optional)

1. In a medium saucepan over medium-high heat, bring the Cauliflower Rice, coconut milk, cinnamon, vanilla, maple syrup, and chia seeds to a boil. Reduce the heat to medium-low and continue to cook until thickened, about 5 minutes.

2. Place the cauliflower oatmeal in a bowl and, if desired, top with strawberries, coconut, hemp seeds, bee pollen, cacao nibs, nut butter, and more maple syrup. Or feel free to use your favorite toppings.

# blue blueberry muffins

I'm a huge fan of sneaking in vitamins and minerals for my kids whenever I can without them necessarily knowing—and definitely without sacrificing any flavor. These muffins are actually blue because of the spirulina. My kids think this is "cool," but little do they know that spirulina is a superfood, offering a major health boost. You can't taste the spirulina. It just makes for fun muffins, which is perfect when hosting a bunch of kids, as I often do.

---

*Makes 16*

—

2 cups plus 2 tablespoons
oat flour

3 teaspoons blue spirulina

1½ teaspoons baking powder

¼ teaspoon baking soda

¼ teaspoon salt

1 cup pure maple syrup

½ cup nut milk of choice
(I like Brazil Nut Milk; page 261)

3 large eggs

1 tablespoon fresh lemon juice

1 teaspoon pure vanilla extract

¼ cup virgin coconut oil,
melted

1 cup fresh blueberries

1. Preheat the oven to 350°F. Prepare a muffin tin with liners.

2. In a large bowl, combine the flour, spirulina, baking powder, baking soda, and salt.

3. In a medium bowl, whisk together the maple syrup, nut milk, eggs, lemon juice, vanilla, and coconut oil until smooth. Add the wet ingredients to the dry ingredients and mix well. Fold in the blueberries until just combined.

4. Pour the batter into the muffin tin, filling each cup about two-thirds of the way. Bake for 20 to 25 minutes, until a toothpick comes out clean. The muffins will keep well in an airtight container on the counter for up to 4 days, or in the fridge for up to 7 days.

# salads

# taco salad
## with spicy cilantro dressing

There's just something wonderful about a hearty taco salad. It has everything I want and need in a meal: veggies for vitamins and minerals, protein to keep me full, rice for comfort, and tons of flavor with the spicy cilantro dressing. Cheese and sour cream round out this salad with the ultimate creaminess. And that's why it is in constant rotation at my house.

---

*Serves 2*

—

½ cup uncooked rice of preference
(I like short-grain brown)

1½ teaspoons extra-virgin olive oil, plus more for drizzling

2½ teaspoons fresh lime juice

½ teaspoon lime zest

1 tablespoon chopped fresh cilantro

Salt and freshly ground black pepper

½ cup chopped tomatoes

½ medium red onion, finely chopped (½ cup)

2 tablespoons avocado oil

1 small yellow onion, thinly sliced

1 green bell pepper, thinly sliced

1 large or 2 small avocados

1 small clove garlic, minced

1. Cook the rice according to the instructions on the package, adding a drizzle of olive oil in the water.

2. In a medium bowl, combine the rice, 1½ teaspoons of the lime juice, the lime zest, and cilantro. Season with salt and pepper, and set aside.

3. In a small bowl, combine the tomatoes, red onion, 1½ teaspoons of the olive oil, and $\frac{1}{8}$ teaspoon salt. Set aside.

4. In a large skillet, warm the avocado oil over medium-high heat. Add the yellow onion, bell pepper, a big pinch of salt, and a small pinch of pepper. Sauté until the onion is translucent and slightly caramelized, 6 to 8 minutes. Remove the skillet from the heat.

5. Meanwhile, make the guacamole: Place the avocado, remaining 1 teaspoon lime juice, $\frac{1}{8}$ teaspoon salt, and garlic in a medium bowl and mash with a fork to combine.

1 large head romaine lettuce, chopped (about 4 cups)

2 Perfectly Cooked Chicken Thighs (page 248), shredded

1 cup grated cheddar cheese

¼ cup sour cream

Spicy Cilantro Dressing (recipe follows)

6. Build the salads: Divide the lettuce between 2 large bowls. Add 1 cup shredded chicken to each bowl, followed by half of the rice, tomato-onion mixture, and green pepper mixture. Top both salads with the cheddar, sour cream, guacamole, and dressing and serve.

# spicy cilantro dressing

*Makes about 1 cup*

—

½ cup plain yogurt

¼ cup fresh lime juice (from 2 to 3 limes)

2 cups packed coarsely chopped fresh cilantro (1 bunch)

1 jalapeño, seeds removed, chopped

3 cloves garlic, coarsely chopped

½ teaspoon ground cumin

½ teaspoon salt

¼ teaspoon freshly ground black pepper

¼ cup extra-virgin olive oil

1. Place the yogurt, lime juice, cilantro, jalapeño, garlic, cumin, salt, and pepper in a high-powered blender. Blend on high until combined, about 20 seconds. Adjust the blender to low and slowly add the olive oil until combined.

2. The dressing will keep well in an airtight container in the fridge for up to 10 days.

# close-to-classic cobb
## with sweet dijon dressing

This salad is a go-to of mine for lunch, but I've also been known to deconstruct it for my kids for dinner. They love eating all the fixings by themselves and I will never not be in the mood for a Cobb salad. I've added roasted asparagus to an otherwise "classic" Cobb, just for an extra green boost.

*Serves 2*

—

8 large stalks asparagus

Extra-virgin olive oil, for drizzling

Salt and freshly ground black pepper

2 large eggs

6 slices bacon

1 large head romaine lettuce, chopped (about 4 cups)

2 Perfectly Cooked Chicken Thighs (page 248), chopped

½ cup chopped cherry tomatoes

½ medium red onion, finely chopped (½ cup)

¾ cup grated cheddar cheese

1 avocado, diced

½ large English cucumber, peeled and chopped (about 1 cup)

Sweet Dijon Dressing (recipe follows)

1. Preheat the oven to 400°F. Line a large baking sheet with parchment paper.

2. Place the asparagus on the prepared baking sheet, drizzle with olive oil, and season with salt and pepper. Roast until bright green, about 5 minutes. Dice, then set aside.

3. Fill a small saucepan with water, set over medium-high heat, and bring to a boil. Carefully place the eggs in the boiling water, turn down to medium-low, and simmer for 9 minutes. Drain, then rinse the eggs with cold water. Set aside and cool for about 5 minutes. Peel the eggs, then dice.

4. Meanwhile, cook the bacon: In a large skillet, cook the bacon in a single layer over medium-high heat, working in batches if needed. Cook until it starts to crisp, about 4 minutes, then flip and cook for another 3 to 4 minutes, until crispy but not burnt. Transfer the bacon to a paper towel–lined plate to blot the excess oil.

5. Build the salads: Divide the lettuce between 2 large bowls. Add half of the eggs, bacon, chicken, tomatoes, onion, asparagus, cheese, avocado, and cucumber to one bowl. Repeat with the remaining ingredients. Drizzle dressing on top of both salads and serve.

*(recipe continues)*

# sweet dijon dressing

*Makes about ½ cup*

—

½ cup extra-virgin olive oil

1 tablespoon fresh lemon juice

2 teaspoons Dijon mustard

½ teaspoon raw honey

½ teaspoon salt

¼ teaspoon freshly ground
black pepper

1. In a medium bowl, whisk together the olive oil, lemon juice, mustard, honey, salt, and pepper until combined.

2. The dressing will keep well in an airtight container in the fridge for up to 10 days.

# greek salad

I went to Greece when I was twenty-four years old and came home and made a Greek salad every day for two weeks straight. I dream about those fresh Greek salads to this day (my favorite part was the massive chunk of feta). I typically have all of these ingredients on hand, making this an easy one to whip up at the last minute.

---

*Serves 2*

—

1 large English cucumber, peeled and chopped

1 cup halved cherry tomatoes

½ small red onion, thinly sliced

½ cup crumbled feta cheese

½ cup kalamata olives, halved and pitted

1 cup garbanzo beans (chickpeas), rinsed and drained

—

**dressing**

3 tablespoons extra-virgin olive oil

1 teaspoon dried oregano

1 teaspoon fresh lemon juice

1 teaspoon apple cider vinegar

2 small cloves garlic, minced

1 teaspoon Dijon mustard

¼ teaspoon salt

Freshly ground black pepper

1. In a large bowl, combine the cucumber, tomatoes, onion, feta, olives, and garbanzo beans.

2. Make the dressing: In a medium bowl, whisk together the olive oil, oregano, lemon juice, vinegar, garlic, mustard, salt, and a pinch of pepper until combined.

3. Pour a little dressing on the salad and mix well. Divide the salad between 2 bowls and drizzle with additional dressing, if desired. Serve immediately.

4. The dressing will keep well in an airtight container in the fridge for up to 10 days.

# salmon blt salad
## with spicy tomatillo ranch dressing

This salad has a few of my favorite things: salmon (which has omega-3s and is so, so good for you), bacon (no explanation needed), avocado (healthy fats), and spicy tomatillo ranch dressing (just *yum*). Together, they create culinary heaven. If you aren't familiar with tomatillos, they're similar to tomatoes but are slightly less sweet and are perfect when drenched in ranch.

---

*Serves 2*

—

1 (1-pound) skin-on
salmon fillet

Extra-virgin olive oil,
for drizzling

Salt and freshly ground
black pepper

1 head butter lettuce,
chopped

¼ small red onion, chopped

1 avocado, diced

1 medium heirloom tomato,
chopped

4 slices bacon, cooked,
chopped

1 tablespoon chopped
fresh chives

Spicy Tomatillo Ranch Dressing
(recipe follows)

1. Preheat the oven to 400°F. Line a small baking sheet with parchment paper.

2. Season the salmon with olive oil, salt, and pepper. Roast the salmon for either 7 to 9 minutes (for a pink and slightly raw center) or 10 to 14 minutes (for a fully cooked center), depending on your texture preference. Remove the skin by scraping it off with a fork. Split the salmon into 2 pieces.

3. Build the salads: Split the lettuce between 2 large bowls. Add half of the onion, avocado, tomato, bacon, and salmon to each bowl. Sprinkle both salads with chives, drizzle with dressing, and serve.

*(recipe continues)*

# spicy tomatillo ranch dressing

*Makes 3 cups*

—

1½ cups mayo

¼ cup full-fat coconut milk

1 tablespoon fresh lime juice

3 tomatillos, coarsely chopped

1 cup packed coarsely
chopped fresh cilantro
(½ bunch)

2 scallions, white and green
parts, coarsely chopped

1 medium clove garlic,
coarsely chopped

2 jalapeños, seeds removed,
coarsely chopped

½ teaspoon salt

Freshly ground black pepper

1. Place the mayo, coconut milk, lime juice, tomatillos, cilantro, scallions, garlic, jalapeños, salt, and a pinch of pepper in a high-powered blender. Blend on high until fully combined, about 30 seconds.

2. The dressing will keep well in an airtight container in the fridge for up to 10 days.

# caesar chicken broccoli salad

I think sun-dried tomatoes are underused in the kitchen. They're sweet-tart and, when done right, they can really make a dish soar. That's exactly what they do here in this yummy but simple salad. Shredded chicken soaks up that creamy Caesar dressing, and the bacon hits all the flavor profiles, plus there's broccoli for a veggie.

*Serves 2*

—

**dressing**

2 small cloves garlic, minced

1 teaspoon anchovy paste

Juice of 1 large lemon (about 2 tablespoons)

1 teaspoon Dijon mustard

1 teaspoon Worcestershire sauce

1 cup mayo

½ cup grated Manchego or Parmesan cheese

¼ teaspoon salt

¼ teaspoon freshly ground black pepper

1 head broccoli, cut into bite-size pieces

2 Perfectly Cooked Chicken Thighs (page 248), shredded

1 cup drained and chopped sun-dried tomatoes

4 slices bacon, cooked, chopped

1. Make the dressing: In a medium bowl, whisk together the garlic, anchovy paste, lemon juice, mustard, and Worcestershire sauce. Add the mayo, Manchego, salt, and pepper and mix well.

2. Make the salad: In a large bowl, combine the broccoli, chicken, tomatoes, and bacon. Pour a little dressing on top and toss to combine. Add more dressing, if desired. Divide the salad between 2 plates and enjoy right away.

3. The dressing will keep well in an airtight container in the fridge for up to 10 days.

# charred cabbage
## with whipped goat's-milk cheese and cucumbers

Let's be honest, you could pair whipped goat's-milk cheese with just about anything, but I like it with the slightly caramelized flavor of charred cabbage and the crunch of Persian cucumbers.

*Serves 2 as a main dish*
*or 4 to 6 as a side*

—

1 medium head purple cabbage

2 tablespoons extra-virgin olive oil, plus more for drizzling

Salt and freshly ground black pepper

1 clove garlic, smashed

8 ounces soft goat's-milk cheese

½ cup plain yogurt

1½ cups packed fresh mint leaves

1½ cups packed fresh parsley leaves

2½ teaspoons fresh lemon juice

3 Persian cucumbers, thinly sliced

Red pepper flakes (optional)

1. Preheat the oven to 450°F. Line a large baking sheet with parchment paper.

2. Cut the cabbage in half through the core, then cut each half into 3 wedges, keeping the core intact. Place the cabbage wedges on the prepared baking sheet, cut-side down. Drizzle the wedges with olive oil and season with salt and pepper. Roast the cabbage for 6 minutes, then turn the wedges onto the other cut side and roast for an additional 6 minutes. Then broil for 5 minutes, until browned and slightly caramelized. Let cool for 5 minutes.

3. Meanwhile, place the garlic, cheese, yogurt, 1 cup of the mint, 1 cup of the parsley, 2 tablespoons olive oil, 1½ teaspoons of the lemon juice, and ½ teaspoon salt in a food processor, and pulse until smooth and light green in color. Transfer the goat's-milk cheese mixture to a medium bowl.

4. In another medium bowl, toss together the cucumbers and the remaining mint, parsley, and lemon juice. Season with salt.

5. To serve, spread a little of the goat's-milk cheese mixture on the bottom of each plate. Add some pieces of cabbage, then top with cucumbers, drizzle with olive oil, and sprinkle with red pepper flakes, if desired.

6. The leftover cheese mixture will keep well in an airtight container in the fridge for up to 5 days.

# arugula salad

## with crispy brussels sprouts
## and honey apple-cider dressing

Yes, fried Brussels sprouts are amazing and I can easily eat them with just a sprinkle of flaky sea salt. But what really makes this dish stand out is the dressing: It's light with the perfect touch of sweetness from honey to balance out the peppery arugula and the smoky fried sprouts. I've been making this dressing for about ten years. The first time was when three of my best friends from LA were visiting me in Chicago. My oldest, Cam, was a little baby then, so we stayed in and cooked dinner. So, this recipe reminds me of that girls' trip and that phase of my life. And truth be told, I need to credit my girls for helping come up with this dressing.

---

*Serves 2*

—

1 bunch (1 pound) Brussels sprouts, trimmed and halved

½ cup avocado oil

Flaky sea salt

3 cups packed chopped arugula

Honey Apple-Cider Dressing (recipe follows)

1 avocado, diced

4 tablespoons pine nuts

1. Fry the Brussels sprouts: In a large Dutch oven, warm the avocado oil over high heat. Once the oil is hot, add the Brussels sprouts and fry, moving occasionally, until golden brown, about 8 minutes. Transfer the Brussels sprouts to a paper towel–lined plate to cool. Sprinkle with flaky sea salt.

2. Place the arugula in a large bowl. Add ¼ cup dressing and toss to coat.

3. Build the salads: Divide the arugula between 2 big bowls. Add half of the Brussels sprouts, half of the avocado, and 2 tablespoons of the pine nuts to each salad. Drizzle additional dressing on top, if desired.

# honey apple-cider dressing

*Makes about 1 cup*

—

3 tablespoons raw honey

¼ cup apple cider vinegar

Juice of 1 large lemon
(about 2 tablespoons)

1 small shallot, minced
(about 2 tablespoons)

½ cup extra-virgin olive oil

Salt and freshly ground
black pepper

1. In a medium bowl, whisk
together the honey, vinegar,
lemon juice, shallot, olive oil,
a big pinch of salt, and a pinch
of pepper until combined.

2. The dressing will keep well
in an airtight container in the
fridge for up to 10 days.

# lobster roll salad
## with dijon dressing

I grew up going to Cape Cod every summer, and one of my favorite memories is getting lobster rolls. Big chunks of lobster slathered in yummy mayo on a buttered bun tasted like legit heaven. Today lobster rolls are a special treat, but I can satisfy my craving with this healthy salad whenever I want.

---

*Serves 2*

—

1 pound cooked lobster meat, coarsely chopped

1 tablespoon fresh lemon juice

¼ cup mayo

2 large stalks celery, finely chopped

2 tablespoons (¼ stick) unsalted butter, melted

2 teaspoons chopped fresh chives, plus more for serving

¼ teaspoon salt

Freshly ground black pepper

1 large head romaine lettuce, chopped (about 4 cups)

1 cup halved cherry tomatoes

Dijon Dressing (recipe at right)

1. In a large bowl, combine the lobster, lemon juice, mayo, celery, butter, chives, salt, and a pinch of pepper.

2. Build the salads: Divide the lettuce between 2 large bowls. Add half of the lobster mixture to each bowl, followed by half of the tomatoes. Drizzle the dressing on top of both salads and sprinkle with extra chives.

## dijon dressing

*Makes about ½ cup*

—

¼ cup extra-virgin olive oil

4 teaspoons Dijon mustard

4 teaspoons fresh lemon juice

Salt and freshly ground black pepper

1. Whisk together the olive oil, mustard, and lemon juice until combined. Season with salt and pepper to taste.

2. The leftover dressing will keep well in an airtight container in the fridge for up to 10 days.

# vegan buffalo cauliflower salad
## with dill ranch dressing

Buffalo sauce will forever be one of my favorites, so it made perfect sense for me to incorporate it into a salad. By now, I think everyone has had buffalo cauliflower, but I still can't get enough. I love it on its own, but I also love it in this salad. Plus, this ranch dressing packs the dill, which is arguably my favorite herb . . . especially when paired with buffalo sauce. For the dressing, you can really use any kind of milk you want, but I like using Brazil Nut Milk (page 261) for the selenium. Selenium is responsible for numerous biological processes, from detoxifying the body to producing hormones.

*Serves 2*

—

3 tablespoons plus 1 teaspoon virgin coconut oil, melted

½ cup oat flour

1 tablespoon garlic powder

½ teaspoon salt

1 head cauliflower, cut into bite-size pieces

½ cup hot sauce (I like Frank's RedHot)

1 large head romaine lettuce, chopped (about 4 cups)

2 large stalks celery, chopped

½ small red onion, thinly sliced

1 avocado, sliced

Chopped fresh dill, for garnish

1. Preheat the oven to 450°F. Grease a large baking sheet with 1 teaspoon of the coconut oil.

2. In a large bowl, whisk together the oat flour, 1 tablespoon of the coconut oil, the garlic powder, salt, and ¼ cup water. Add the cauliflower and toss to coat. Place the cauliflower on the prepared baking sheet and bake for 15 minutes.

3. In another large bowl, combine the hot sauce and the remaining 2 tablespoons coconut oil. Add the cauliflower and toss to coat. Place the cauliflower back on the baking sheet and roast for an additional 25 minutes, until golden brown.

4. Meanwhile, make the dill ranch dressing: Place the mayo, nut milk, vinegar, parsley, onion powder, garlic powder, dill, and pepper in a high-powered blender and blend on high until smooth, 30 to 45 seconds.

### dill ranch dressing

1½ cups mayo

¼ cup nut milk, such as Brazil Nut Milk (page 261)

1 tablespoon apple cider vinegar

1 tablespoon chopped fresh parsley

1½ teaspoons onion powder

1 teaspoon garlic powder

2 teaspoons chopped fresh dill

¾ teaspoon freshly ground black pepper

5. To serve, divide the lettuce between 2 large bowls. Add half of the cauliflower, celery, onion, and avocado to each bowl. Drizzle both salads with dressing and top with dill.

6. The extra dressing will keep well in an airtight container in the fridge for up to 10 days.

# chopped niçoise salad

I had never heard of this salad until I was twenty and living in LA, and I had a business lunch with my manager, who is still my manager to this day. I didn't know how to pronounce *Niçoise* and instead said something to the effect of "ni-coize." She made sure to immediately correct me. I have never forgotten that moment of complete embarrassment, but I also found a new favorite salad, so I guess it was not a total loss. And now I know Niçoise salad is named after the city of Nice in France . . . Who knew?

---

*Serves 2*

—

¾ pound red potatoes

Extra-virgin olive oil, for coating

Salt and freshly ground black pepper

4 large eggs

¾ pound green beans

1 teaspoon avocado oil

1 pound fresh tuna

2 medium tomatoes, coarsely chopped

1 cup kalamata olives

1 (15-ounce) can garbanzo beans (chickpeas), rinsed and drained

1 medium English cucumber, peeled and chopped

1. Preheat the oven to 425°F. Line a large baking sheet with foil.

2. Coat the potatoes with olive oil and season with salt and pepper. Place the potatoes on the prepared baking sheet and roast for 25 minutes, until fork-tender. Let cool slightly, then chop.

3. Meanwhile, make the dressing: In a small bowl, whisk together the mustard, garlic, vinegar, olive oil, 1 teaspoon salt, and 1 teaspoon pepper until combined. Set aside.

4. Fill a small saucepan with water, set over medium-high heat, and bring to a boil. Gently add the eggs and cook for 9 minutes. Drain, then run the eggs under cold water. Let cool slightly, then peel and cut in half.

5. Meanwhile, fill a large saucepan with water, set over medium-high heat, and bring to a boil. Blanch the green beans in the boiling water for 2 minutes, until they're bright green in color. Run the green beans under cold water, then drain and cut in half.

### dressing

1½ teaspoons Dijon mustard

5 cloves garlic, minced

1½ tablespoons red wine vinegar

¼ cup plus 3 tablespoons extra-virgin olive oil

Salt and freshly ground black pepper

6. In a large skillet, warm the avocado oil over high heat. Season the tuna with salt and pepper. Sear the tuna for 1 minute on each side, until lightly browned on the outside. Transfer the tuna to a cutting board and cut it into ½-inch slices.

7. To serve, arrange the potatoes, eggs, green beans, tuna, tomatoes, olives, garbanzo beans, and cucumber in a row on a large serving platter. Drizzle the salad with the dressing, as desired, and serve.

8. The extra dressing will keep well in an airtight container in the fridge for up to 10 days.

# lunch

# loaded quesadillas

Quesadillas are the meal I like to fall back on when I haven't had time to run to the grocery store or when I'm just feeling unmotivated to make an involved dinner. I always have the basics for quesadillas on hand, and I know I can count on my kids to gobble them up. This recipe calls for chicken thighs, but you can use whatever leftover cooked chicken you have in the fridge, and it will still taste great.

---

*Serves 4*

—

1 tablespoon avocado oil, plus more for coating

1 red bell pepper, thinly sliced

½ medium yellow onion, thinly sliced

Salt

1 cup grated cheddar cheese

8 tortillas (I like the Siete brand almond flour)

1 (15-ounce) can black beans, rinsed and drained

2 Perfectly Cooked Chicken Thighs (page 248), thinly sliced

Sour cream, for serving

—

**guacamole**

1 avocado

½ teaspoon fresh lime juice

Salt

1. In a large skillet, warm the avocado oil over medium heat. Add the bell pepper, onion, and a pinch of salt. Sauté until the onion is translucent, about 5 minutes, then remove the skillet from the heat.

2. Spread ¼ cup of the cheddar over 1 tortilla. Add one-quarter of the pepper-onion mixture, followed by one-quarter of the beans, and one-quarter of the chicken. Place another tortilla on top. Repeat with the remaining ingredients to make 3 more quesadillas.

3. Warm a large skillet over medium heat. Lightly coat with avocado oil. Place a quesadilla inside and cook until it is golden brown and the cheese starts to melt, about 5 minutes. Flip the quesadilla and cook the other side an additional 3 to 4 minutes, until the cheese is completely melted.

4. Make the guacamole: In a small bowl, mash together the avocado, lime juice, and a pinch of salt until combined.

5. To serve, cut each quesadilla into quarters and serve with a dollop each of sour cream and guacamole.

# shrimp ceviche

Ceviche is always my first meal by the pool on a beach vacation. I love that it's light, yet filling, and packed with flavor. During the warm months, I make ceviche at home about once a week. This recipe is a touch sweet with the orange juice and has a hint of heat with the jalapeño. I eat ceviche with a fork for a meal, but it's also good with chips and can be a yummy appetizer.

*Serves 2*

—

18 large shrimp (about 1 pound), peeled, deveined, and chopped

¼ cup fresh lemon juice (from about 2 lemons)

¼ cup fresh orange juice

¼ cup fresh lime juice (from 2 to 3 limes)

1 jalapeño, seeds removed, finely chopped

½ cup chopped cherry tomatoes

2 Persian cucumbers, chopped

¼ small red onion, finely chopped

¼ cup finely chopped fresh cilantro

1 avocado, diced

Salt and freshly ground black pepper

1. In a large bowl, combine the shrimp, lemon juice, orange juice, and lime juice. Let sit for 15 minutes. Discard as much liquid as you can by tilting the bowl over the sink (it's okay if some juice is left in the bowl).

2. Add the jalapeño, tomatoes, cucumbers, onion, cilantro, and avocado to the shrimp and season with salt and pepper. Mix well.

3. Serve right away or let chill for 30 minutes to 1 hour.

# crab cakes

I like my crab cakes classic, just a touch of creaminess so the crab really shines and isn't overpowered by spices. Everyone tries to put their own spin on crab cakes, but this is a time when I say: "If it ain't broke, don't fix it." Serve these with the Bacon-Wrapped Asparagus (page 188).

---

*Makes 6*

—

2 large eggs

¼ cup mayo

2 teaspoons Dijon mustard

2 teaspoons Worcestershire sauce

¼ teaspoon salt

2 tablespoons chopped fresh parsley

1 pound lump crabmeat, drained

½ cup panko breadcrumbs

Avocado oil, for the pan

6 lemon wedges, for serving

1. In a large bowl, combine the eggs, mayo, mustard, Worcestershire, salt, and parsley. Add the crab and breadcrumbs and fold to incorporate. Place the crab mixture in the fridge for 15 minutes. Once it's chilled, shape the crab mixture into 6 cakes.

2. Coat a large skillet with avocado oil and set over medium heat. Cook the crab cakes for 3 to 5 minutes, until golden brown. Carefully flip and cook an additional 3 to 4 minutes on the other side.

3. Enjoy the crab cakes right away with lemon wedges or save any leftovers, as they'll keep well in the fridge for up to 2 days.

# vegan veggie rice bowls
## with sweet tahini dressing

This bowl is so warm and comforting. I like saving extra dressing and throwing it on salads or dipping roasted veggies in it.

---

*Serves 2*

—

1 small sweet potato, coarsely chopped

1 cup broccoli bite-size florets

½ small red onion, diced

8 ounces Brussels sprouts, trimmed and halved

2 large carrots, peeled and chopped

1 tablespoon plus 1½ teaspoons extra-virgin olive oil, plus more for the pan

Salt

½ bunch Lacinato kale, ribs and stems removed, then chopped

2 cups cooked rice of choice (I like black forbidden rice)

—

**sweet tahini dressing**

3 tablespoons extra-virgin olive oil

1 tablespoon pure maple syrup

2 tablespoons tamari

2 tablespoons tahini

1 clove garlic, coarsely chopped

1. Preheat the oven to 400°F. Line a large baking sheet with foil.

2. In a large bowl, toss the sweet potato, broccoli, onion, Brussels sprouts, and carrots with 1 tablespoon of the olive oil, and season with salt. Transfer the coated vegetables to the prepared baking sheet and roast until tender, 30 to 35 minutes.

3. Meanwhile, warm the remaining 1½ teaspoons olive oil in a skillet over medium heat. Sauté the kale with a pinch of salt until wilted, about 2 minutes.

4. Make the sweet tahini dressing: Place the olive oil, maple syrup, tamari, tahini, garlic, and 2 tablespoons water in a high-powered blender and blend until smooth. Set aside.

5. To build the bowls: Place 1 cup of the rice in the bottom of 2 bowls. Add half of the veggies to each bowl and drizzle with the dressing. Enjoy immediately.

# teriyaki chicken bowls

I made this bowl specifically for my middle kid, Jaxon. He loves bowls in general but every time we go out for sushi, he orders a teriyaki bowl instead. Teriyaki sauce can be loaded with sugar, so I've substituted honey as the sweetener.

---

*Serves 4*

—

2 cups broccoli florets

Extra-virgin olive oil, for coating

Salt

4 boneless skinless chicken thighs, cubed

4 cups cooked rice, such as short-grain brown rice

1 medium English cucumber, peeled and chopped

4 scallions, white and green parts, sliced

Toasted sesame seeds, for garnish

Seaweed Crumble (page 258)

—

**teriyaki sauce**

½ cup tamari

¼ cup raw honey

2 tablespoons rice vinegar

1 teaspoon sesame oil

1 teaspoon grated fresh ginger

2 small cloves garlic, minced

1 tablespoon arrowroot powder

1. Preheat the oven to 400°F. Line a large baking sheet with parchment paper.

2. In a large bowl, coat the broccoli with olive oil and season with salt. Transfer the broccoli to the prepared baking sheet and roast until slightly charred, 30 to 35 minutes.

3. Meanwhile, in another large bowl, coat the chicken with olive oil. In a large skillet over medium heat, sauté the chicken until cooked through, 5 to 6 minutes.

4. Meanwhile, make the teriyaki sauce: In a medium saucepan, combine the tamari, honey, rice vinegar, sesame oil, ginger, garlic, arrowroot powder, and ½ cup water. Whisk the teriyaki sauce over medium-high heat until it is thickened, about 5 minutes. Add the sauce to the chicken and stir to combine.

5. To build the bowls: Place 1 cup of the rice in the bottom of 4 bowls. Add one-quarter of the chicken with sauce to each bowl, followed by one-quarter each of the broccoli, cucumber, and scallions. Garnish the bowls with sesame seeds and Seaweed Crumble and serve.

# sushi bowls two ways

I introduced my kids to sushi at a young age, so they've never really known any different . . . they love it. I'm giving you two ways to do a sushi bowl, one with salmon and one with scallops. I first had raw scallops about two years ago and they immediately became my favorite. They're sweet and creamy . . . and they melt in your mouth. For kids who don't like fish, substitute cooked chicken thighs. I do that for Jaxon from time to time, since the older he's gotten, the more he won't go near fish. This recipe calls for a spiralizer, which I highly recommend using, but if that's not an option, you could thinly slice the zucchini on a mandoline. Or, honestly, you could just leave it out!

## salmon bowl

*Serves 2*

—

1 pound skinless salmon

Virgin coconut oil, melted, for coating

Salt and freshly ground black pepper

2 cups cooked rice, such as black forbidden rice

1 medium English cucumber, peeled and chopped

1 small zucchini, spiralized

1 avocado, diced

¼ cup sushi ginger

Seaweed Crumble (page 258)

Spicy Mayo (page 263)

Tamari and/or ponzu

1. Preheat the oven to 375°F. Line a medium baking sheet with parchment paper.

2. On the prepared baking sheet, coat the salmon with coconut oil and season with salt and pepper. Bake for 8 minutes (if you like the center rare), or up to 12 minutes (if you prefer it fully cooked).

3. To build the bowls: Place 1 cup of the rice in the bottom of 2 bowls. Add half the salmon, cucumber, zucchini, and avocado to each bowl. Top both bowls with sushi ginger, Seaweed Crumble, and Spicy Mayo, and drizzle with tamari and/or ponzu sauce. Enjoy immediately.

*(recipe continues)*

# scallop bowl

*Serves 2*

—

### dressing

¼ cup coconut aminos

Juice of 1 lime
(about 2 tablespoons)

½ teaspoon grated
fresh ginger

1 tablespoon toasted
sesame oil

½ teaspoon toasted
sesame seeds

4 large raw scallops

2 cups cooked rice such as
black forbidden rice

1 medium English cucumber,
peeled and chopped

2 scallions, white and green
parts, sliced

1 habanero chile (optional),
seeds removed, thinly sliced

Seaweed Crumble (page 258)

1. Make the dressing: In a medium bowl, whisk together the coconut aminos, lime juice, ginger, sesame oil, and sesame seeds.

2. Pat the scallops dry with a paper towel. Slice each scallop crosswise into thin layers.

3. To build the bowls: Place 1 cup of the rice in the bottom of a bowl. Add half of the scallops followed by half of the cucumber, scallions, and, if desired, habanero chile. Repeat with the remaining ingredients in another bowl. Top both bowls with the Seaweed Crumble and drizzle with the dressing. Enjoy immediately.

# cauliflower risotto
## with garlic shrimp

Risotto can be very heavy, even though it's incredibly delicious. In my opinion, the best part of risotto is how creamy the rice gets. Well, what if I told you it's possible to achieve that creaminess with cauliflower? Cauliflower is one of my favorite veggies to cook with because of its versatility. It is so mild that it takes on whatever flavor you want, plus it can get super creamy and luxurious, just like normal risotto. Certainly, the cheeses help with the creamy texture, but the cauliflower completely replaces the rice for a healthier option.

---

*Serves 2 as a main dish*
*or 4 as a side*

—

1 tablespoon extra-virgin olive oil

1 medium yellow onion, minced

2 cloves garlic, minced

3 cups Cauliflower Rice (page 260)

1½ cups vegetable broth

½ bunch Lacinato kale, ribs and stems removed, then chopped (1 cup)

Salt and freshly ground black pepper

1. In a large skillet, warm the olive oil over medium heat. Add the onion and cook until translucent, about 4 minutes. Add the garlic and cook for 30 seconds, until aromatic. Add the Cauliflower Rice and broth and bring to a boil. Reduce the heat to medium-low and simmer for 8 minutes, until the liquid has evaporated. Remove the skillet from the heat.

2. Make the sauce: Transfer 2 cups of the cooked Cauliflower Rice to a high-powered blender. Add the coconut milk and blend until smooth. Add the cheddar, Manchego, salt, and lemon juice. Blend until smooth.

3. Add the kale to the remaining cauliflower in the skillet. Cook over low heat until the kale is wilted, 1 to 2 minutes. Pour the sauce on top of the kale-cauliflower mixture and stir to combine. Season with salt and pepper to taste. Keep the cauliflower risotto on low heat while you cook the shrimp.

*(recipe and ingredients continue)*

**sauce**

1 cup full-fat coconut milk

1 cup grated white cheddar
cheese

¼ cup grated Manchego or
Parmesan cheese

1 teaspoon salt

Juice of 1 large lemon
(about 2 tablespoons)

—

**shrimp**

1 tablespoon unsalted butter

2 cloves garlic, minced

1 pound large shrimp, peeled,
deveined, and tails removed

½ teaspoon paprika

½ teaspoon red pepper flakes,
plus more (optional) for
serving

Salt

4. Cook the shrimp: In another large
skillet, melt the butter over medium-
high heat. Add the garlic and cook for
30 seconds, until aromatic. Add the
shrimp, paprika, red pepper flakes,
and a big pinch of salt. Cook for 3 to
4 minutes, then flip and cook another
2 to 3 minutes, until the shrimp are no
longer opaque.

5. To serve, divide the cauliflower
risotto between 2 bowls. Top with the
shrimp and sprinkle with additional
red pepper flakes, if desired.

# cheesy chicken–stuffed poblanos

These poblano chiles have all the delicious, traditional flavors you would expect in a Mexican dish, but cumin is the standout. I use chicken thighs in most of my recipes because they have way more flavor than breasts, but you could, of course, use chicken breasts instead. I've found that most men love stuffed peppers (not really sure what that's about!), so make this when you want to impress any man in your life.

*Serves 2*

—

2 large poblano chiles

1 tablespoon unsalted butter

2 Perfectly Cooked Chicken Thighs (page 248), shredded

½ teaspoon chili powder

2 tablespoons ground cumin

½ teaspoon smoked paprika

1 teaspoon garlic powder

½ teaspoon onion powder

Salt and freshly ground black pepper

4 ounces sour cream

1 cup grated cheddar cheese

Chopped fresh cilantro, for garnish

1. Preheat the oven to 350°F. Line a large baking sheet with foil.

2. Cut the peppers in half lengthwise and discard the seeds. Set aside.

3. Melt the butter in a large skillet over medium heat. Add the chicken, chili powder, cumin, paprika, garlic powder, onion powder, a big pinch salt, and a pinch of pepper. Sauté until the flavors combine, about 1 minute. Remove the skillet from the heat and stir in the sour cream.

4. Stuff each pepper with the chicken mixture. Place the stuffed peppers on the prepared baking sheet, open-side up. Sprinkle ¼ cup of the cheddar on each pepper half.

5. Bake for 15 to 20 minutes, until the cheese is melted.

6. Serve the stuffed peppers warm, with a sprinkle of cilantro on top.

# mexican pizza

Before I committed to a healthy lifestyle, Taco Bell was my weakness (through high school and in my early twenties). No matter what, my order was always a Mexican Pizza. When I heard Taco Bell discontinued their Mexican Pizza, I knew I had to re-create it (yes, they've since brought it back by popular demand!). Since we all know I won't be going there, now I can still relive those younger years without hurting my body.

*Serves 4*

—

½ pound ground beef

1 medium yellow onion, chopped (¾ cup)

2 cloves garlic, minced

1 teaspoon chili powder

1 teaspoon ground cumin

¾ teaspoon salt

½ teaspoon freshly ground black pepper

8 tortillas (I like the Siete brand almond flour)

1 (16-ounce) can refried beans

2 cups grated cheddar cheese

½ cup salsa

1 large tomato, chopped

2 scallions, white and green parts, chopped

¼ cup sour cream

1. Preheat the oven to 350°F. Line a large baking sheet with parchment paper.

2. In a large skillet, sauté the beef, onion, and garlic over medium heat until the beef is browned and the onion is tender, about 4 minutes. Stir in the chili powder, cumin, salt, and pepper. Remove the skillet from the heat.

3. Place 4 of the tortillas on the prepared baking sheet. Cover each with one-quarter of the refried beans and one-quarter of the beef mixture, then top with another tortilla. Bake for 12 minutes. Remove the baking sheet from the oven and sprinkle the top of each pizza with ½ cup of the cheddar. Then add 2 tablespoons salsa, one-quarter of the tomatoes, and one-quarter of the scallions to each. Bake for another 8 minutes, until the cheese is melted.

4. To serve, dollop 1 tablespoon sour cream on top of each pizza. Enjoy warm.

# chicken skewers
## with bang bang sauce

This recipe uses my go-to marinade—it's good on chicken, salmon, and beef. Coconut aminos is similar to soy sauce in that it has loads of umami flavor, but is milder and a touch sweeter. This chicken is good all on its own, but the Bang Bang Sauce is what takes it to the next level for me. Spicy, creamy, and sweet, it has all of my favorite flavors in one sauce. In Chinese street food, Bang Bang Sauce is traditionally paired with fried chicken, so this recipe is definitely healthier. If you don't have chicken tenders, you can cut boneless, skinless chicken thighs into one-inch strips.

---

*Serves 4*

—

2 pounds chicken tenders

2 tablespoons extra-virgin olive oil

1 teaspoon paprika

1 teaspoon garlic powder

Salt and freshly ground black pepper

¼ cup coconut aminos

—

**bang bang sauce**

½ cup mayo

1 teaspoon coconut aminos

1 teaspoon raw honey

½ teaspoon garlic powder

2½ tablespoons Sriracha

1. Place the chicken tenders in a large bowl. Add 1 tablespoon of the olive oil, the paprika, and garlic powder and season with salt and pepper. Thread the tenders on 4 skewers.

2. Warm the remaining 1 tablespoon olive oil in a large skillet or grill pan over medium-high heat. Add the chicken tenders and cook for 6 minutes. While they're cooking, pour 2 tablespoons of the coconut aminos over the top. Flip the chicken and cook them an additional 6 to 8 minutes, pouring the remaining 2 tablespoons coconut aminos over the top.

3. Meanwhile, make the Bang Bang Sauce: In a large bowl, whisk together the mayo, coconut aminos, honey, garlic powder, and Sriracha until smooth.

4. To serve, either drizzle the sauce directly on the chicken tenders or divide it among 4 small bowls to be used as a dipping sauce.

# panfried zucchini pizza

This zucchini-crust pizza is healthy and satisfies my pizza craving. I've included this pesto version here but you could also do a more classic version with tomato sauce, spinach, tomatoes, mozzarella, and basil.

---

*Serves 2*

—

1 medium zucchini, grated

½ cup chickpea flour

½ teaspoon garlic powder

½ teaspoon dried oregano

Salt and freshly ground black pepper

1½ teaspoons extra-virgin olive oil, plus more for coating and drizzling

2 cups packed spinach

3 tablespoons Pesto (page 254)

1 tomato, thinly sliced

2 ounces soft goat's-milk cheese

Red pepper flakes

¼ cup packed fresh basil leaves

1. Preheat the oven to 400°F. Line a medium baking sheet with parchment paper.

2. Place the grated zucchini in a cheesecloth or dish towel and squeeze out the extra moisture over the sink. Transfer the zucchini to a large mixing bowl. Add the chickpea flour, garlic powder, oregano, ¼ teaspoon salt, a pinch of pepper, and ½ cup water and mix well.

3. Warm a medium (10-inch) frying pan over medium heat. Coat with olive oil. Transfer the zucchini dough to the pan, then spread it out by tapping or pushing it until it touches the edges. Turn up the heat to medium-high and fry the dough for 8 minutes, until the bottom is crispy. Flip the dough and cook the other side an additional 5 minutes. Using a metal spatula, transfer the crust onto the prepared baking sheet, being careful not to break it.

4. Warm the 1½ teaspoons olive oil in a large skillet pan over medium heat. Add the spinach and a pinch of salt and sauté until wilted, about 2 minutes. Remove the pan from the heat.

5. Spread the pesto on the pizza. Place the spinach all around the pizza and top it with the tomato and goat's-milk cheese. Sprinkle with red pepper flakes, place the basil leaves all around, and drizzle olive oil on top.

6. Bake for 10 to 15 minutes, until the cheese is melted. Serve immediately.

# tacos two ways

I've never met anyone who doesn't like tacos, and I've never had a taco I didn't like. I've got two different versions here: a heartier carne asada option that resembles simple street tacos, and a lighter shrimp tacos option (with a bonus cabbage veggie).

## carne asada

*Serves 6 to 8*

—

2 tablespoons tamari

Juice of 1 lime
(about 2 tablespoons)

2 tablespoons avocado oil

3 cloves garlic, minced

2 teaspoons chili powder

1 teaspoon ground cumin

Salt and freshly ground black pepper

1½ pounds skirt steak, cut into ¼-inch slices

12 to 16 tortillas (I like the Siete brand almond flour)

1 small white onion, chopped (¾ cup)

½ cup chopped fresh cilantro

1 avocado, sliced, for serving

1. In a medium bowl, whisk together the tamari, lime juice, 1 tablespoon of the avocado oil, the garlic, chili powder, cumin, a big pinch of salt, and a big pinch of pepper. Pour the marinade into a zip-top bag with the steak and marinate for 30 minutes, or up to overnight.

2. Heat the remaining 1 tablespoon avocado oil in a large skillet over medium heat. Add the steak and all of the marinade and cook, stirring often, until the steak is browned and the marinade is reduced, about 5 minutes. Add another pinch of salt, stir to combine, and remove the skillet from the heat.

3. In a large skillet over medium heat, warm the tortillas for about 30 seconds, working in batches.

4. To serve, place some steak on each warmed tortilla, then add some onion, cilantro, and avocado. Serve immediately.

# tequila lime shrimp with cabbage slaw

*Serves 6 to 8*

—

1½ pounds large shrimp, peeled, deveined, tails removed, and halved lengthwise

Salt and freshly ground black pepper

1 tablespoon avocado oil

2 cloves garlic

1 tablespoon minced canned chipotle chiles in adobo sauce

2 scallions, white and green parts, thinly sliced

⅓ cup blanco tequila

1 teaspoon lime zest

12 to 16 tortillas (I like the Siete brand almond flour)

Grated white cheddar cheese

—

**cabbage slaw**

¼ medium head green cabbage, shredded (about 2½ cups)

2 cloves garlic, coarsely chopped

½ cup sour cream

Juice of 1 lime (about 2 tablespoons)

4 scallions, white part only, coarsely chopped

½ cup chopped fresh cilantro

Salt

1. In a large bowl, pat the shrimp dry with paper towels and season with salt and pepper.

2. Heat the avocado oil in a large skillet over medium heat. Add the garlic, chiles, scallions, and ¼ teaspoon salt. Cook until softened, about 2 minutes. Add the tequila and simmer until it has evaporated and the pan is dry, about 5 minutes. Add the shrimp and cook, stirring often, until it is cooked through and no longer opaque, 3 to 5 minutes. Transfer the shrimp mixture to a large bowl and stir in the lime zest. Set aside.

3. Make the cabbage slaw: Place the cabbage in a large bowl.

4. Place the garlic, sour cream, lime juice, scallions, cilantro, and a big pinch of salt in a high-powered blender. Blend on high until smooth. Pour the sauce over the cabbage and toss to coat.

5. In a large skillet over medium heat, warm the tortillas for about 30 seconds, working in batches.

6. To serve, place some of the shrimp mixture on a tortilla, followed by the cabbage slaw. Top with some cheddar. Repeat with the remaining ingredients. Serve immediately.

# air fryer chicken nuggets
## with chick-fil-a–inspired sauce

I've only ever had Chick-fil-A once in my life, but those chicken nuggets were amazing. I wanted to re-create them at home, so I didn't have to go get fast food. Someone once told me that Chick-fil-A's secret is that their chicken marinates in pickle juice. I don't know if that's true or not, but these are really dang good. I use boneless chicken thighs for maximum flavor. This recipe also uses an air fryer, but if you don't have one, no problem. You can fry them in avocado oil.

*Serves 4 to 6*

—

1 pound boneless skinless chicken thighs, cut into 1-inch pieces

1 cup dill pickle juice

¾ cup whole milk or full-fat coconut milk

1 large egg

¼ cup raw honey

1 cup cassava flour

1¼ teaspoons salt

1 teaspoon paprika

1 teaspoon garlic powder

Avocado oil spray

Chick-fil-A–Inspired Sauce (recipe follows), for serving

1. In a large bowl, submerge the chicken thighs in pickle juice, making sure all of the chicken is covered. Transfer the bowl to the fridge and marinate for at least 15 minutes, or up to overnight.

2. Set the air fryer to 400°F.

3. In a medium bowl, whisk together the milk, egg, and honey until smooth. Set aside.

4. In a large bowl, combine the flour, salt, paprika, and garlic powder.

5. Drain the chicken thighs. Coat each piece of chicken with the flour mixture, then submerge it in the milk mixture, then dredge it in the flour mixture again, making sure to wipe off any excess between each mixture.

*(recipe continues)*

6. Spray each piece of chicken with avocado oil spray to make sure they get crispy. Cook the chicken in a single layer, not touching, for 9 minutes, until golden brown, flipping halfway through.

7. If you don't have an air fryer, you can fry the chicken in avocado oil in a large skillet over medium heat. Working in batches, fry each piece of chicken until it is golden brown and cooked through, 4 to 5 minutes per side. Transfer the cooked chicken to a paper towel–lined plate to blot the excess oil.

8. Serve the chicken nuggets alongside Chick-fil-A–Inspired Sauce for dipping.

# chick-fil-a–inspired sauce

*Makes about 1 cup*

—

¼ cup raw honey

2 tablespoons yellow mustard

¼ cup your favorite BBQ sauce

1 teaspoon apple cider vinegar

½ cup mayo

½ teaspoon garlic powder

½ teaspoon paprika

1. In a medium bowl, whisk together the honey, mustard, BBQ sauce, vinegar, mayo, garlic powder, and paprika until well combined.

2. The sauce will keep well in an airtight container in the fridge for up to 10 days.

# steak tartare

I went back and forth about whether I should include this recipe in the cookbook or not. I wanted to include it because steak tartare is truly my favorite thing on the planet, but I also realize you need really good-quality meat to make this recipe, and not everyone has access to that. I did a poll on my Instagram and it was literally split fifty-fifty, so I made the call to give it to you. Also, don't let raw beef be the only reason you don't try this! It melts in your mouth, it's so tender and delicious. This also makes for a great app at a house party.

---

*Serves 2*
—

14 ounces good-quality raw
beef tenderloin,
finely chopped

1 shallot, finely chopped

2 tablespoons chopped
fresh parsley

1 good-quality egg yolk

—

**double mustard dressing**

3 tablespoons extra-virgin
olive oil

2 teaspoons Dijon mustard

2 teaspoons whole-grain
mustard

1 tablespoon red wine vinegar

1 teaspoon capers, chopped

Salt and freshly ground
black pepper

1. In a large bowl, combine the beef, shallot, and parsley.

2. Make the double mustard dressing: In a medium bowl, whisk together the olive oil, both mustards, vinegar, and capers until well combined. Season with salt and pepper to taste.

3. To serve, place the beef tartare on a plate. Place the egg yolk in the middle on top of the beef. Drizzle the dressing to taste over the top. Mix the egg yolk in with the beef mixture when you're ready to eat.

# beef and broccoli bowls

My favorite dish growing up was Chinese beef and broccoli. Since my family and I love bowls, I decided to turn that dish into a bowl. Plus, my daughter, Saylor, would eat soba noodles at every meal, if I let her. So when I tell her soba noodles are in a dish, she's all in. I use buckwheat soba noodles here, since they're gluten-free and still hearty, but go ahead and use your favorite.

---

*Serves 2*

—

1 (8-ounce) package buckwheat soba noodles

1 pound flank steak, cut into ¼-inch slices

1 tablespoon plus ⅓ cup avocado oil

1 teaspoon arrowroot powder

1 medium head broccoli, cut into bite-size pieces

Extra-virgin olive oil, for drizzling

Salt and freshly ground black pepper

2 scallions, white and green parts, chopped

Red pepper flakes, for garnish

Toasted sesame seeds, for garnish

1. Cook the noodles according to the directions on the package, then drain and rinse to prevent them from sticking together. Set aside.

2. Preheat the oven to 400°F. Line a large baking sheet with parchment paper.

3. Place the steak in a large zip-top bag with 1 tablespoon of the avocado oil and the arrowroot powder. Massage to combine. Let sit for 5 minutes.

4. Spread out the broccoli on the prepared baking sheet. Drizzle it with olive oil and sprinkle it with a couple of pinches each of salt and pepper. Roast the broccoli for 20 to 25 minutes, until it is slightly charred.

5. Meanwhile, make the sauce: In a small saucepan, warm the avocado oil over medium heat. Add the garlic and ginger and sauté until fragrant, 30 seconds or so. Whisk in the tamari, broth, and coconut sugar. Bring the sauce to a boil, then simmer until it thickens, about 10 minutes.

6. Meanwhile, in a large skillet, warm the remaining ⅓ cup avocado oil over medium-high heat. Sear the steak in a single layer for 1 minute on each side until browned, then transfer it to a paper towel–lined plate. Reduce the heat to low and

### sauce

1 tablespoon avocado oil

2 cloves garlic, minced

½ teaspoon grated fresh ginger

¼ cup tamari

⅓ cup beef broth

¼ cup coconut sugar

discard any excess oil. Transfer the steak back to the pan, add half of the sauce, and cook it for 1 minute, until the flavors combine. Remove the skillet from the heat.

7. Transfer the noodles to a large bowl. Add the remaining sauce and toss to combine.

8. To build the bowls: Divide the noodles between 2 serving bowls. Add half of the beef, broccoli, and scallions to each bowl, then garnish with red pepper flakes and sesame seeds. Serve immediately.

# dinner

# simple balsamic-glazed
# sea bass with roasted tomatoes

This recipe was inspired by one of my longest friendships. A group of girls who I've been friends with since I was 18 took a beach vacation along Scenic Highway 30A in Florida, and Charlene made a variation of this one night. I wrote everything down and made it as soon as I got home. I changed it up slightly, but my girl is the real brains behind this one. Hands down, this is the recipe to make when you want to impress your guests without having to put in too much effort. The sea bass is melt-in-your-mouth good and the balsamic glaze is my new favorite go-to when I want a dish that seems elevated but doesn't take forever in the kitchen.

---

*Serves 4*

—

4 cups cherry tomatoes, halved

4 tablespoons extra-virgin olive oil

Salt and freshly ground black pepper

4 sea bass fillets (6 to 8 ounces each)

6 teaspoons your favorite store-bought balsamic glaze

6 tablespoons chopped fresh basil

Flaky sea salt, for garnish

1. Preheat the oven to 450°F. Line two large baking sheets with foil.

2. Place the cherry tomatoes on the prepared baking sheet. Pour 2 tablespoons of the olive oil on top of the tomatoes, add 2 big pinches of salt, and toss with your hands to combine. Roast the tomatoes for 30 to 35 minutes, until blistered.

3. Meanwhile, place the sea bass on the second prepared baking sheet. Drizzle the remaining 2 tablespoons olive oil on top and season with salt and pepper. Bake for 20 to 25 minutes, until the fish starts to flake.

4. To serve, place 1 sea bass fillet on each plate. Drizzle ½ teaspoon of the balsamic glaze and spoon some tomatoes on top of each fillet. Then place 1½ tablespoons basil on each fillet and drizzle each with 1 teaspoon of the balsamic glaze. Finally, garnish each portion with a small pinch of flaky sea salt on top.

5. Enjoy right away.

# baked ziti
## with sausage and kale

A pasta bake checks a lot of boxes for me: They're easy, they're full of flavor, they typically make a ton, so I can usually count on leftovers, and my kids love them. I'm a big fan of throwing spinach or kale in a pasta bake because you really can't taste it, but you get the health benefits (can you tell by now that I love getting extra greens in whenever possible?!). This baked ziti has all the classic Italian flavors—ricotta for the creaminess, oregano (which reminds me of cooking with my Italian dad), and, of course, marinara sauce and mozzarella. When making this recipe, I've used both regular ricotta and buffalo ricotta. Both work great, but I prefer buffalo, since we try to avoid cow's milk for the most part.

*Serves 6*

—

2 teaspoons extra-virgin olive oil, plus more for the pan

1 (8-ounce) package ziti

1 pound Italian sausage, casing removed, crumbled

1 medium yellow onion, finely chopped (about 1½ cups)

4 cloves garlic, minced

1 bunch Lacinato kale, ribs and stems removed, then chopped (4 cups)

1 (10-ounce) container whole-milk ricotta

1 large egg, lightly beaten

1 teaspoon dried oregano

1. Preheat the oven to 350°F. Coat a 9 × 13-inch baking dish with olive oil.

2. Cook the ziti according to the directions on the package, but stop 1 minute before they're fully cooked. Drain the ziti.

3. Meanwhile, heat the olive oil in a large skillet over medium heat. Add the sausage and cook, breaking up any big pieces, until it starts to brown, about 5 minutes. Add the onion and garlic and cook for another 5 minutes, until the onion is tender. Add the kale and cook until wilted, 1 to 2 minutes. Transfer the sausage mixture to a large bowl.

4. Add the cooked pasta, ricotta, egg, oregano, salt, pepper, and ¼ cup of the marinara sauce to the sausage mixture, and mix well.

½ teaspoon salt

½ teaspoon freshly ground black pepper

1 (25-ounce) jar of your favorite marinara sauce

8 ounces mozzarella cheese, grated

5. Spread ¼ cup of the marinara sauce on the bottom of the prepared baking dish. Top with half of the pasta mixture, half of the remaining marinara sauce, and half of the grated cheese. Repeat the layers.

6. Cover the baking dish with foil and bake for 20 minutes. Uncover and bake until the cheese is melted, 5 to 8 minutes. Let cool 10 minutes before serving.

# tex-mex casserole

This dish is similar to the popular Shredded Chicken Enchilada Casserole in my cookbook *True Comfort,* but with a few variations: Instead of enchilada sauce, I use chicken broth and sour cream to make it creamier and lighter, and I don't use any beans in this recipe. I love casseroles because they make a ton of food, are easy to freeze for later use, are always full of flavor, and are relatively painless to make.

---

*Serves 6 to 8*

—

Avocado oil, for the pan

6 tablespoons (¾ stick) unsalted butter

1 medium yellow onion, chopped (about 1½ cups)

1 red bell pepper, diced

2 medium poblano chiles, chopped (about 1 cup)

1 jalapeño, seeds removed, chopped

2 cloves garlic, minced

1 tablespoon chili powder

1 tablespoon ground cumin

1 teaspoon salt

½ teaspoon freshly ground black pepper

¼ cup oat flour

1¾ cups chicken broth

1 (10-ounce) can diced tomatoes with green chiles, drained

1. Preheat the oven to 375°F. Grease a 9 × 13-inch baking dish with avocado oil. Set aside.

2. Melt the butter in a large skillet over medium-high heat. Add the onion, bell pepper, poblano chiles, and jalapeño. Cook, stirring occasionally, until the vegetables are softened, about 8 minutes. Stir in the garlic, chili powder, cumin, salt, and pepper. Cook for 1 minute, until the flavors combine.

3. Sprinkle the flour over the veggie mixture and stir to combine. Whisk in the broth and turn the heat up to high. Bring to a boil, stirring constantly, until thickened, 1 to 2 minutes. Remove the skillet from the heat. Stir in the tomatoes and sour cream.

4. In a large bowl, combine the chicken and cilantro. Add the veggie mixture and mix well.

5. Warm a large skillet over high heat. Lightly grease with avocado oil. Cook the tortillas until golden brown and crispy, 1 to 2 minutes per side, working in batches. Transfer them to a large baking sheet or large plate.

1 cup sour cream

5 Perfectly Cooked Chicken
Thighs (page 248), chopped

1 cup chopped fresh cilantro

18 tortillas (I like the Siete
brand almond flour)

1½ cups grated cheddar
cheese

6. Line the baking dish with 6 tortillas, overlapping them slightly, to cover the bottom. Top with half of the chicken mixture and one-third of the cheddar. Repeat the chicken and cheddar layers. Top with the remaining tortillas and cheddar.

7. Cover and bake for 20 minutes. Uncover and bake for 10 minutes, until bubbling and lightly browned on top. Let cool for 10 minutes before serving.

8. The casserole will keep well in the fridge for up to 7 days or in the freezer for up to 6 months.

# enchiladas verdes

This recipe will always have a very special place in my heart because it was in the initial book proposal that I put together before I had ever written a book. I pitched my first cookbook with about twenty recipes, and this was one of them. It didn't end up making it into my first few books, so I'm really excited to finally include it. The reason it didn't make it in my first cookbook, *True Roots,* was because I felt it was too heavy, and the reason it didn't make it into *True Comfort* was because I was being super mindful of how much dairy I was including in that book (and I ended up going with the Shredded Chicken Enchilada Casserole instead). But I really do love these enchiladas (the tomatillo sauce makes them special) and I love making them when my kids have friends over, since they make a lot and are a crowd fave. It's been my tried-and-true recipe for a big group for years now.

---

*Serves 4 to 6*

—

**salsa**

Coconut oil, for the pan

12 tomatillos, quartered

½ jalapeño, seeds removed, chopped

½ medium yellow onion, coarsely chopped

2 cloves garlic

1 teaspoon ground cumin

2 tablespoons extra-virgin olive oil, plus more for drizzling

¼ cup chopped fresh cilantro

½ teaspoon salt

1 teaspoon fresh lime juice

1. Make the salsa: Preheat the oven to 425°F. Lightly coat an 8 × 8-inch baking dish with coconut oil.

2. Place the tomatillos, jalapeño, onion, garlic, and cumin in the prepared baking dish and drizzle with a little olive oil, then use your hands to combine the mixture. Roast the tomatillos for 35 to 40 minutes, or until they are soft and starting to brown. Let them cool for a few minutes.

3. Place the cooked veggie mixture in a high-powered blender. Add the cilantro, olive oil, salt, and lime juice. Starting on low and working your way up to high, blend the mixture until it is smooth, about 45 seconds. Set aside.

4. Make the enchiladas: Warm the coconut oil in a large skillet over high heat. Add the bell pepper, onion, and jalapeño.

*(recipe and ingredients continue)*

## enchiladas

1 tablespoon virgin coconut oil

1 yellow bell pepper, thinly sliced

½ medium yellow onion, thinly sliced

½ jalapeño, seeds removed, minced

1 teaspoon ground cumin

1 teaspoon paprika

½ teaspoon salt

2 tablespoons chopped fresh cilantro

2 Perfectly Cooked Chicken Thighs (page 248), thinly sliced

8 tortillas (I like the Siete brand almond flour)

16 ounces buffalo mozzarella, torn into small pieces

Sauté until the peppers are soft and the onion is caramelized, 8 to 10 minutes. Add the cumin, paprika, and salt and cook for 1 to 2 minutes, until the cumin is aromatic. Remove the skillet from the heat and stir in the cilantro. Add the chicken and ¼ cup of the salsa and mix well.

5. Warm the tortillas in a large skillet over medium-high heat, for about 30 seconds each, working in batches. Keep them warm inside a dry kitchen towel.

6. Turn the oven down to 375°F.

7. Make an assembly line: warm tortillas, a big plate, the chicken filling, and the 9 × 13-inch baking dish. Pour ¼ cup of the salsa onto the plate. Pour another ¼ cup of the salsa on the bottom of the baking dish, spreading it out to lightly coat.

8. Take 1 of the warm tortillas and dip it in the salsa to lightly coat both sides. Add about ¼ cup of the chicken filling and roll it up. Place the filled enchilada in the baking dish, seam-side down. Repeat with the remaining tortillas. If you have extra filling, squeeze it into any open spaces in the baking dish. Pour any remaining salsa (about ¾ cup) over the top and sprinkle the enchiladas with the buffalo mozzarella.

9. Cover and bake for 20 minutes. Uncover and bake for another 10 to 15 minutes, until the cheese is melted and bubbling.

10. Let cool 10 minutes before serving.

11. The enchiladas will keep well in the fridge for up to 7 days or in the freezer for up to 6 months.

# beef stroganoff

Beef Stroganoff reminds me of my uncle John. He made this all the time when I stayed with my cousins growing up. I always remember loving it so much, but for whatever reason, my parents never made it. So I decided to re-create it for my own family. I was so excited to make this for my kids the first time, really hoping they would love it like I did. Luckily, they did. Beef Stroganoff is a Russian dish and people over the years have created many different variations, but I like mine the classic way. To make this gluten-free, use a gluten-free fettuccine and either gluten-free all-purpose flour or oat flour.

---

*Serves 4*

—

1 (8-ounce) package fettuccine

3 tablespoons unsalted butter

3 tablespoons avocado oil

8 ounces white button mushrooms, trimmed and chopped

Salt and freshly ground black pepper

12 ounces beef tenderloin, cut into ⅛-inch strips

¾ cup dry red wine

1 medium yellow onion, minced (about 1¾ cups)

1½ teaspoons coconut sugar

1 teaspoon tomato paste

2 tablespoons all-purpose flour

1. Cook the noodles according to the directions on the package, stopping 1 minute before they're fully cooked. Drain and rinse the noodles, then return them to the pot. Add 2 tablespoons of the butter and cover to keep warm.

2. Warm 2 tablespoons of the avocado oil in a large skillet over medium-high heat. Cook the mushrooms with ¼ teaspoon salt until they are browned and tender, about 5 minutes. Transfer the mushrooms to a large bowl and set aside.

3. Pat the beef dry with a paper towel. Season it with salt and pepper.

4. Heat the remaining 1 tablespoon avocado oil in the same large skillet over medium heat. Cook the beef, stirring frequently, until it is brown on both sides, about 5 minutes. Add the beef to the bowl with the mushrooms.

5. Add ¼ cup of the wine to the same large skillet over medium-high heat. Scrape up any brown bits while bringing

*(recipe and ingredients continue)*

¾ cup chicken broth

⅓ cup sour cream

¼ cup chopped fresh parsley,
for garnish

the wine to a boil. Reduce the heat
to medium-low and simmer for
2 minutes to reduce the wine. Add
the sauce to the bowl with the
mushrooms and beef.

6. In the same large skillet over
medium-high heat, add the remaining
1 tablespoon butter. Add the onion,
coconut sugar, and tomato paste.
Cook until the flavors combine and
the onion is soft, about 5 minutes.

7. Stir in the flour until combined.
Add the broth and the remaining
½ cup wine. Simmer until thickened,
about 2 minutes. Add any juices
that have accumulated in the beef-
mushroom mixture. Stir in the sour
cream until combined. Add the beef
and mushrooms and season with salt
and pepper.

8. To serve, place the noodles in a
dish, spoon the beef-mushroom sauce
on top, and garnish with parsley.

# stuffed spaghetti squash boats

These stuffed boats are light, and they let the squash, sausage, and veggies speak for themselves. When I'm in the mood for a little extra flavor, I love putting a couple big spoonfuls of pesto (see page 254) on mine. The presentation is fun, since they are served in the shells, which makes them great for a crowd. Just be careful not to puncture the shells when you're scraping out the spaghetti squash!

*Serves 4*

—

2 medium spaghetti squash, halved and seeds removed

1 teaspoon plus 1 tablespoon extra-virgin olive oil, plus more for coating

Salt and freshly ground black pepper

1 pound Italian sausage, casing removed

1 small yellow onion, chopped

3 cloves garlic, minced

2 medium zucchini, chopped

2 medium tomatoes, chopped

2 cups packed spinach, chopped

2 cups grated Manchego cheese

1. Preheat the oven to 400°F. Line a large baking sheet with foil.

2. Place the squash on the prepared baking sheet and coat with olive oil, then season with salt and pepper. Roast the squash, cut-side down, for 45 minutes, until fork-tender.

3. Meanwhile, warm 1 teaspoon of the olive oil in a large skillet over medium heat. Sauté the sausage, breaking it up, until browned, about 3 minutes. Transfer the sausage to a large bowl.

4. In the same large skillet, warm the remaining 1 tablespoon olive oil over medium heat. Add the onion and sauté for 1 minute, until it softens slightly. Add the garlic and cook for another minute, until aromatic. Add the zucchini, tomatoes, and a pinch of salt and sauté until the vegetables are tender, about 3 minutes. Add the spinach and sauté until wilted, 30 to 45 seconds. Remove the skillet from the heat and transfer the vegetables to the same bowl as the sausage.

5. Scrape the squash into the bowl with the sausage and veggies, being careful not to poke any holes in the shell. Mix well. Spoon the mixture into the squash shells until they just barely overflow. Top each shell with ½ cup of the Manchego. Bake for 5 to 6 minutes, until the cheese is melted. Serve right away.

# slow-cooker
# buffalo chicken casserole

I've realized how short life is and that everything is about moderation, so if I want some dang cream cheese from time to time, so be it. This recipe is still relatively healthy even with the cream cheese, since it uses cauliflower rice and has broccoli in it. This recipe is keto-friendly, for those who like to eat that way. Once you get the slow cooker going, you really just need thirty minutes to get everything else ready.

---

*Serves 4 to 6*

—

1 bottle of your favorite buffalo sauce (I like Primal Kitchen)

1½ pounds boneless, skinless chicken thighs (about 6 large thighs)

1½ cups broccoli florets

1 teaspoon extra-virgin olive oil, plus more for drizzling

Salt and freshly ground black pepper

2 cups Cauliflower Rice (page 260)

1 (8-ounce) tub cream cheese

1. Turn the slow cooker on low (if you want to cook for 8 hours) or high (if you want to cook for 4 hours). Place about ¼ cup buffalo sauce on the bottom of the bowl. Add the chicken, then pour the remaining sauce on top. Cover and cook.

2. About 30 minutes before your time is up, start the veggies.

3. Preheat the oven to 425°F. Line a large baking sheet with parchment paper.

4. Place the broccoli on the prepared baking sheet, then drizzle with some olive oil and season with salt and pepper. Roast the broccoli for 15 to 20 minutes, until golden brown. Remove the baking sheet from the oven.

5. Heat the olive oil in a large skillet over medium-high heat. Add the Cauliflower Rice, a pinch of salt, and a pinch of pepper and sauté for 5 minutes, until the cauliflower starts to get a little tender. Remove the skillet from the heat.

6. Once the chicken is done cooking, use 2 forks to shred it in the slow cooker. Add the Cauliflower Rice and the cream cheese and stir to combine. Add the broccoli and season with salt and pepper to taste. Cook for 10 to 15 minutes for the flavors to combine.

# creamy prosciutto pasta

You can throw prosciutto in just about any pasta dish to make it really good—I stand by this! I'm half kidding, but it really does seem like all the good pasta dishes out there have prosciutto in them. I don't eat a lot of pork, but I definitely make an exception for dishes like this. Creamy and ever-so-slightly salty, with the cheeses and prosciutto, this dish is actually fairly light, making it perfect to eat with a glass of white wine on the screened-in porch on a warm summer night.

---

*Serves 4*

—

1 (8-ounce) package elbow pasta

¼ cup (½ stick) unsalted butter

1 large yellow onion, finely chopped (about 2 cups)

⅓ cup dry white wine

1 cup full-fat coconut milk

½ cup soft goat's-milk cheese

1 cup grated Manchego cheese

Salt and freshly ground black pepper

1 teaspoon extra-virgin olive oil, plus more for drizzling

8 slices prosciutto, chopped

1 tablespoon chopped fresh parsley, for garnish

1. Cook the pasta according to the directions on the package, then drain.

2. Meanwhile, melt the butter in a large skillet over medium heat. Add the onion and sauté until translucent, about 5 minutes. Add the wine and cook until it has evaporated, about 6 minutes. Add the coconut milk, goat's-milk cheese, and ½ cup of the Manchego, whisking to combine. Season with salt and pepper. Bring the sauce to a boil, then turn down to medium-low and simmer. Add the cooked pasta and stir to combine.

3. In a medium skillet, warm the olive oil over medium-high heat. Cook the prosciutto until it is crispy, 8 to 10 minutes. Transfer the prosciutto to a paper towel–lined plate to blot the excess oil.

4. Add the prosciutto to the pasta and mix well. Season with salt and pepper to taste. Spread the remaining ½ cup Manchego over the top of the pasta, then cover and let sit for 5 to 6 minutes, until the cheese begins to melt.

5. To serve, drizzle with olive oil and garnish with the parsley.

# grilled lamb skewers

Skewers automatically make me think of summer, which is when I can grill barefoot (my favorite way to cook). Lamb has a very distinct flavor—a lot of people say it's gamy but still really delicious. To be honest, I also just like changing it up so we aren't always eating chicken or beef. You can let the lamb marinate for up to eight hours, but what's so great about these skewers is how fast and easy they can be. They're still flavorful with only a few minutes of marinating. And they are great served with Tzatziki Sauce (page 251).

---

*Serves 6*

—

1 cup plain yogurt

1 tablespoon ground cumin

2 cloves garlic, minced

Juice of 1 large lemon (about 2 tablespoons)

Salt and freshly ground black pepper

1½ pounds leg of lamb, cut into 1½-inch pieces

Avocado oil, for the grill or grill pan

1. In a medium bowl, whisk together the yogurt, cumin, garlic, lemon juice, 1 teaspoon salt, and ½ teaspoon pepper. Place the lamb in the mixture and toss to coat. Let the lamb sit for 5 minutes.

2. Thread the lamb pieces onto 6 skewers, then place on a large plate. Season with salt and pepper.

3. Lightly grease a grill or grill pan with 1 teaspoon oil over high heat. Position the skewers on the grill and cook for 8 minutes. Flip and cook for an additional 4 to 6 minutes (for medium rare) or more, as desired. Let rest for 10 minutes before serving.

# greek chicken and artichokes

My dad inspired this recipe. The kids and I went to stay with him in Colorado to go skiing, and he made a similar dish for us. I loved that it was a one-pot meal, it didn't take long, and all of my kids enjoyed it. This dish is also really healthy, and if you keep artichoke hearts on hand, like I do, it can be easily thrown together without a premeditated meal plan.

*Serves 4*

—

9 tablespoons extra-virgin olive oil

¼ cup fresh lemon juice (from about 2 lemons)

6 cloves garlic, minced

2 teaspoons dried oregano

8 bone-in, skin-on chicken thighs

Salt and freshly ground black pepper

2 (10-ounce) cans artichoke hearts, drained

1. In a large bowl, whisk together 4 tablespoons of the olive oil, the lemon juice, garlic, and oregano. Add the chicken and toss to coat, making sure to get some marinade under the skin. Let the chicken marinate for 10 minutes, or up to overnight.

2. Warm a skillet large enough to fit the chicken in a single layer over medium-high heat, working in batches if needed. Coat with 2 tablespoons of the olive oil.

3. Season the chicken with a few big pinches of salt and a pinch of pepper. Once the skillet is hot, place the chicken in, skin-side down. Pour the remaining marinade over the top. Sear the chicken, covered, until it is golden brown, about 10 minutes.

4. Flip the chicken, add the artichoke hearts, and drizzle with the remaining 3 tablespoons olive oil. Cook for an additional 7 minutes, uncovered, until the chicken is cooked through and the artichokes are golden brown and a little caramelized.

# one-pot
# cod bake

A one-pot recipe is a working parent's dream. This pasta bake has a slightly smoky flavor, with the smoked paprika, which pops in combination with the dill. I think it's a really yummy but unexpected pairing. Cod is one of my favorite fish. It's light and mild, so it just takes on whatever flavors you want it to. I love throwing veggies in a pasta bake because it's obviously an easy way for my kids and me to get some greens in. I typically use a gluten-free shell pasta, or even a lentil pasta, but feel free to use your own favorite.

*Serves 4*
—

1 teaspoon extra-virgin olive oil, plus more for drizzling

1 small yellow onion, finely chopped (about 1 cup)

Salt and freshly ground black pepper

2 cloves garlic, minced

1 teaspoon smoked paprika

1 small head broccoli, cut into bite-size pieces

1½ cups vegetable broth

1 (8-ounce) package shell pasta

¼ cup chopped fresh dill

¾ cup frozen peas

1 (½-pound) skinless cod fillet

Red pepper flakes (optional)

1. Preheat the oven to 400°F.

2. Heat the olive oil in a deep, ovenproof frying pan over medium heat. Add the onion and sauté until soft, 5 to 6 minutes. Add 1 teaspoon salt, ½ teaspoon pepper, and the garlic and cook for 1 minute, until fragrant. Add the paprika, broccoli, and broth and stir to combine. Bring to a boil, then stir in the pasta.

3. Cover the frying pan, transfer it to the oven, and bake the pasta mixture for 15 minutes. Remove the frying pan from the oven and stir in the dill and peas. Add the cod, nestling it in the middle of everything. Drizzle with a little olive oil.

4. Cover the frying pan, return it to the oven, and bake for 8 to 10 minutes, until the fish is cooked through and the pasta is tender. Season with salt and pepper to taste.

5. To serve, sprinkle the cod bake with red pepper flakes, if desired.

# creamy feta halibut

Halibut is a wonderful mild whitefish that can essentially take on any flavor. It's perfect with the feta in this ultimate creamy dish. I like pairing this dish with a lighter side, like roasted asparagus or Roasted Broccoli with Anchovy Breadcrumbs (page 175).

---

*Serves 4*

—

4 halibut fillets (6 to 8 ounces each), skin removed

Salt and freshly ground black pepper

4 tablespoons extra-virgin olive oil

1 small shallot, thinly sliced

2 cloves garlic, minced

1 tablespoon chopped fresh thyme

1 cup full-fat coconut milk

¾ cup crumbled feta cheese

1. Season the halibut with salt and pepper. Warm 2 tablespoons of the olive oil in a large skillet over medium heat. Cook the halibut for 3 to 5 minutes on each side, or until cooked through. Remove the skillet from the heat and set aside.

2. In a small saucepan, warm the remaining 2 tablespoons olive oil over medium heat. Add the shallot and sauté until fragrant, about 2 minutes. Add the garlic and thyme and cook for 1 to 2 minutes, until aromatic. Whisk in the coconut milk and feta until combined, about 45 seconds. Turn the heat to medium-low and simmer until thickened and creamy, about 5 minutes. Remove the saucepan from the heat and season with ½ teaspoon salt and ½ teaspoon pepper.

3. To serve, spoon the feta sauce over the halibut. Enjoy right away.

# dairy-free tuscan spaghetti squash casserole

I try to be mindful of how much dairy we eat in my house, so I always get excited about dairy-free sauce that's still creamy and delicious. Cashews are the nondairy lover's best friend in this regard. They can make just about anything creamy without bringing any weird flavor to the dish. This casserole is light because it uses spaghetti squash, it has a green with the spinach, and it won't weigh you down since it's gluten- and dairy-free—so it's an easy and healthy weeknight meal. The only part that's time-consuming is cooking the squash, but I like to get other things done while it roasts (that's a good time to unpack the kids' lunch boxes from school, put away any dishes, et cetera).

---

*Serves 6*

—

1 large spaghetti squash, halved and seeds removed

Extra-virgin olive oil, for drizzling

Salt and freshly ground black pepper

1 pound mild Italian chicken sausage, casing removed

4 cups spinach, chopped

1. Preheat the oven to 400°F. Line a large baking sheet with foil.

2. Drizzle the squash with olive oil and season with salt. Place the squash cut-side down on the prepared baking sheet and roast for 45 to 50 minutes, until it is fork-tender. Remove the baking sheet from the oven (but keep the oven on).

3. Prep for the sauce: Place the cashews in a medium bowl and completely cover with hot water. Soak for 10 minutes, then drain and rinse.

4. Meanwhile, in a large skillet over medium-high heat, cook the sausage, breaking it up, until the meat is browned, 4 to 6 minutes. Remove the skillet from the heat.

*(recipe and ingredients continue)*

### sauce

1 cup cashews

2 cloves garlic, coarsely chopped

½ cup full-fat coconut milk

1 tablespoon fresh lemon juice

1 teaspoon salt

¼ teaspoon freshly ground black pepper

½ teaspoon red pepper flakes

5. Make the sauce: Place the soaked cashews, garlic, coconut milk, lemon juice, salt, pepper, red pepper flakes, and ¾ cup water in a high-powered blender. Blend on high until smooth, 30 to 45 seconds.

6. Using a fork, scrape the cooked spaghetti squash into a large bowl. Pour the cashew sauce on top. Add the cooked sausage and stir to combine. Fold in the spinach and stir until it has wilted, about 30 seconds. Season with salt and pepper.

7. Transfer the mixture to a baking dish and bake for 15 minutes.

8. Serve warm.

# restaurant-style lobster tails

This is the recipe to make when you want to impress a date, your family, or even just your friends. These lobster tails will look like you ordered them at the fanciest restaurant, but they're really so simple. The key is being deliberate about where you cut the shell and pull out the lobster meat, and making sure the meat is still attached at the bottom of the tail.

---

*Serves 2*

—

2 large lobster tails

¼ cup (½ stick) salted butter

¼ teaspoon paprika

¼ teaspoon garlic powder

Salt and freshly ground black pepper

1. Preheat the oven to 450°F. Line a large baking sheet with parchment paper.

2. Position the lobster tails on a cutting board with the shell-sides facing up and the lobster tails pointed away from you. Using sharp kitchen shears, cut the top of each lobster tail down the middle of the back toward the tail.

3. Flip over both lobster tails and carefully separate the meat from the shell by simultaneously pulling up the middle of the shell with one hand while pressing down on the meat with the fingers of your other hand. Flip the lobster tails back over, slowly and carefully pulling up the lobster meat in one piece. The meat should still be attached at the bottom of the tail. Place the lobster tails on the prepared baking sheet and set aside.

4. In a small saucepan, melt the butter over medium heat. Whisk in the paprika, garlic powder, a pinch of salt, and a pinch of pepper.

5. Brush the lobster meat with the butter mixture until it is well coated.

6. Bake for 12 to 15 minutes, until the meat is cooked through. Serve right away.

# nobu's black cod

Black cod is also known as "butterfish" for its intense buttery flavor and velvety texture. This is one of my favorite recipes in the whole book and if you've ever had the black cod at the famous restaurant Nobu, then you know why. Nobu is easily one of my favorite restaurants for their unique take on traditional Japanese cuisine. I could dedicate an entire cookbook to recipes I've created inspired by what I've eaten at Nobu, but this cod is hands-down my favorite. I like serving this dish with Cucumber Sunomono Salad (page 194) and Miso Scallion Noodles (page 186).

---

*Serves 2*

—

2 tablespoons mirin

2 tablespoons sake

¼ cup white miso paste

2 tablespoons pure maple syrup

2 skinless cod fillets (6 to 8 ounces each)

Avocado oil, for the grill pan

1. In a small saucepan over medium-high heat, combine the mirin and sake and bring to a boil. Add the miso paste and stir until it has dissolved. Then add the maple syrup and cook, turning the heat down to medium-low heat, whisking continuously for 1 to 2 minutes, until the flavors are combined. Remove the saucepan from the heat to cool slightly.

2. Once the marinade has cooled, place the cod fillets in a large zip-top bag, add the sauce, and gently massage to coat the fish. Place the zip-top bag in the fridge to marinate for 15 minutes, or up to 3 days.

3. When you're ready to eat, preheat the oven to 400°F. Line a medium baking dish with parchment paper.

4. Warm a little avocado oil on a grill pan over high heat. Once the oil is hot, scrape the excess marinade off the fish, then place it on the grill pan. Cook for 2 minutes, until browned. Flip the fish and cook the other side for 2 minutes, until browned.

5. Transfer the fish to the prepared baking dish and bake for 12 to 18 minutes, until the fish is flaky. Serve right away.

# citrus salmon
## with chili oil

This recipe has become a regular in my house and has gotten me out of my cooking rut with salmon (sometimes I get stuck always making it the same way over and over). I love how light this recipe is, and the mild citrus flavor instantly transports me to warm summer nights. I could pour this chili oil on just about anything, and if you like spicy stuff, like I do, I suggest really loading it on. Also, don't be afraid to use a decent amount of flaky sea salt—salt is your best cooking friend, and I would argue it makes or breaks a dish (plus, good-quality salt has a ton of minerals and is actually good, and necessary, for us!).

---

*Serves 4*
—

1 medium fennel bulb, thinly sliced

1 blood orange, thinly sliced

1 lemon, seeds removed and thinly sliced

1 lime, seeds removed and thinly sliced

4 sprigs fresh dill, plus more for serving

¼ cup extra-virgin olive oil

Salt and freshly ground black pepper

1 (2-pound) skinless salmon fillet, deboned

2 tablespoons Chili Oil (page 253), plus more for drizzling

Flaky sea salt

1. Preheat the oven to 350°F.

2. Place the fennel, orange, lemon, lime, and dill in a shallow baking dish big enough to hold the salmon (you can cut the salmon in half or into 4 fillets, if needed). Pour the olive oil over the top of the fennel and citrus slices and season them with salt and pepper, using your hands to combine everything.

3. Season the salmon with salt and pepper. Place the salmon on top of the fruit mixture. Pour the Chili Oil over the top of the fillet and season with another pinch of salt.

4. Bake for 22 to 25 minutes (if you like the center rare), or longer as desired.

5. To serve, place a portion of the salmon on a plate and spoon some of the fruit mixture on top. Drizzle with chili oil and sprinkle with dill and flaky sea salt.

# sweet balsamic chicken thighs

I'm constantly trying to find new ways to change up chicken. I'm sure you all are, too. My family gets bored with it, but luckily we all love this recipe. It's ever-so-slightly sweet, which balances the mellow tartness of the balsamic vinegar. It also has the perfect amount of creaminess without feeling heavy. Open up a nice bottle of red wine with this one and serve it with Sour Cream and Chive Potato Salad with Crispy Shallots (page 192) and Roasted Carrots with Manchego (page 197).

*Serves 4*

—

8 large bone-in, skin-on chicken thighs

Salt and freshly ground black pepper

1 teaspoon garlic powder

2 tablespoons avocado oil

¼ cup (½ stick) unsalted butter

¼ cup dry white wine

¾ cup finely chopped shallots (about 2 medium)

1 teaspoon fresh chopped thyme

2 teaspoons coconut sugar

4 teaspoons balsamic vinegar

1 cup chicken broth

1 cup full-fat coconut milk

1 tablespoon arrowroot powder

1. Place the chicken on a baking sheet and season with salt, pepper, and the garlic powder.

2. Heat the avocado oil in a large skillet over medium-high heat. Once the oil is hot, place the chicken in the pan, skin-side down, and cook it until the skin crisps, 6 to 7 minutes. Flip the chicken and cook 5 minutes, or until the internal temperature reaches 165°F. Transfer the chicken to a plate. Set aside.

3. In the same large skillet, melt the butter over medium-low heat. Add the wine and shallots and cook until the shallots are translucent, 8 to 10 minutes, scraping up any brown bits. Add the thyme, coconut sugar, and balsamic vinegar and cook for 4 minutes, stirring occasionally, until the flavors have combined.

4. Add the broth and bring to a boil. Turn the heat down to low and simmer for 2 to 3 minutes, until the sauce thickens slightly. Add the coconut milk, a pinch of salt, and a pinch of pepper and stir to combine.

*(recipe continues)*

5. Dissolve the arrowroot powder in a small bowl with 1 tablespoon water, then whisk to combine. Add the dissolved arrowroot to the sauce, whisking continuously until it is fully combined and the sauce has thickened slightly.

6. Place the chicken thighs in the sauce, skin-side up, and simmer on medium-low heat for 8 minutes. Flip the thighs and cook for 8 to 12 minutes, until the chicken is cooked through.

7. To serve, spoon the sauce over the chicken.

# panfried chicken
## with spicy arugula and honey mustard

Fried chicken is always a favorite, especially when it's fried in healthier options, like avocado oil, and breaded with cassava flour. Avocado oil doesn't cause inflammation, as do a lot of other oils that chicken is typically fried in. And cassava flour is made from cassava root, which is a root vegetable and is gluten-free. I leave out the arugula for my kids (they won't go near it) and just give myself the extra. Turmeric is a powerful anti-inflammatory, so I love including it when I can.

---

*Serves 4 to 6*

—

1½ pounds boneless, skinless chicken thighs (about 6 large thighs)

1 cup cassava flour

1 teaspoon paprika

½ teaspoon garlic powder

¼ teaspoon onion powder

1 teaspoon ground turmeric

Salt and freshly ground black pepper

2 large eggs

½ cup avocado oil

2 cups arugula, coarsely chopped

1 teaspoon extra-virgin olive oil

⅛ teaspoon cayenne pepper

1. Preheat the oven to 375°F. Line a large baking sheet with parchment paper.

2. Using a kitchen mallet, pound the chicken thighs until they're about ¼ inch thick.

3. In a medium shallow dish, combine the cassava flour, paprika, garlic powder, onion powder, turmeric, 2 teaspoons salt, and ¼ teaspoon pepper.

4. In another medium shallow dish, beat the eggs until they're slightly frothy.

5. Coat each chicken thigh with egg, then dredge it in the flour mixture, making sure to wipe off any excess egg or flour mixture in between. Place the coated chicken thighs on the prepared baking sheet.

*(recipe and ingredients continue)*

**honey mustard**

¼ cup raw honey

¼ cup plus 3 tablespoons
stone-ground mustard

1 tablespoon fresh lemon juice

¼ cup mayo

1 teaspoon paprika

¼ teaspoon garlic powder

6. Warm the avocado oil in a large skillet over medium-high heat. Once the oil is hot, place the thighs in the pan in a single layer, working in batches if needed. Fry the thighs for 2 to 3 minutes, until golden brown. Flip the thighs and cook on the other side for 2 to 3 minutes, until golden brown. Place the fried chicken back on the prepared baking sheet.

7. Bake for 10 minutes, until the chicken is cooked through.

8. Meanwhile, in a large bowl, toss the arugula with the olive oil, a big pinch of salt, a pinch of black pepper, and the cayenne pepper. Set aside.

9. Make the honey mustard: In a small bowl, whisk together the honey, mustard, lemon juice, mayo, paprika, and garlic powder until fully combined.

10. To serve, place a chicken thigh on each plate. Top with the arugula and drizzle with the honey mustard.

# meatless spinach cashew ricotta lasagna

This lasagna is meatless, and I make it as a side dish for a big group of people, but it can of course be the main dish for a meatless night or for all of my vegetarians. This cashew ricotta recipe is from my first cookbook, *True Roots,* and I could eat it by the spoonful—it's that good. Lasagna will always be one of my most comforting dishes, so I also like making this on rainy nights when the kids and I are just gonna be cozy on the couch. I like freezing leftovers in individual servings, so I can just pull them out as needed.

*Serves 6 to 8*

—

### cashew ricotta

1 cup raw cashews

2 egg yolks

1 cup grated Manchego cheese

1 cup packed fresh basil leaves

1 teaspoon lemon zest

2 cloves garlic, coarsely chopped

½ cup extra-virgin olive oil

½ teaspoon salt

1. Place the cashews in a large bowl. Completely cover the cashews with hot water and soak for 15 minutes, then drain and rinse.

2. Cook the noodles according to the directions on the package, then drain.

3. Preheat the oven to 350°F.

4. Make the cashew ricotta: Place the soaked cashews, egg yolks, Manchego, basil, lemon zest, garlic, olive oil, salt, and ½ cup water in a high-powered blender. Blend until smooth and paste-like.

5. Heat the olive oil in a large skillet over medium heat. Add the garlic and sauté until aromatic, about 30 seconds. Add the spinach and cook until wilted, about 1 minute.

1 (9-ounce) package
lasagna noodles

4 teaspoons extra-virgin
olive oil

4 small cloves garlic, minced

10 cups spinach, coarsely
chopped

1 (25-ounce) jar of your
favorite marinara sauce

7 ounces buffalo mozzarella,
torn into small pieces

6. Pour a little pasta sauce, about ½ cup, on the bottom of a
9 × 9-inch baking dish. Put a layer of the cooked noodles
on top of the sauce (one-third of the noodles), followed by
one-third spinach, one-third cashew ricotta, and more pasta
sauce. Repeat the layers. Top with the buffalo mozzarella.

7. Bake for 45 to 50 minutes, until the cheese is melted and
slightly golden brown. Let the lasagna cool for 10 minutes
before serving.

# new york strip steak

I never took the time, or really ever needed to know how, to perfectly cook a steak until I became single. But then I committed to figuring it out. I wanted to be well versed in all things steak—to be able to grill it, pan sear it, and finish it in the oven, or to just cook it on the stove top. And I did just that. I make these strips at least twice a week—we love steak at my house. I like my steak medium rare, but feel free to cook it longer for well done or your personal preference (although I would strongly encourage you to go the medium-rare route). I don't use any salt in this recipe, since coconut aminos are salty already, but you could also just liberally season the steak with salt and pepper and sear it in butter. If you have really good-quality meat, sometimes that's all you need.

---

*Serves 2*

—

¼ cup liquid coconut aminos

2 large cloves garlic, minced

1 teaspoon Dijon mustard

Freshly ground black pepper

2 New York strip steaks
(6 to 8 ounces each)

Unsalted butter, for the pan

1. In a small bowl, whisk together the coconut aminos, garlic, mustard, and a big pinch of pepper.

2. Place the steaks in a large zip-top bag. Pour the marinade over the top of the steaks and massage to coat. Let the steaks sit on the counter for 15 minutes, or place them in the fridge for up to overnight.

3. When you're ready to eat, preheat the oven to 400°F. Line a medium baking sheet with parchment paper.

4. Warm a large skillet over medium-high heat. Once the skillet is hot, coat it with butter. Sear the steaks for 2 minutes, until they are slightly browned. Flip the steaks and sear the other side for 2 minutes, until they are slightly browned. Transfer the steaks to the prepared baking sheet.

5. Bake for 9 to 10 minutes (for medium rare), or longer if desired.

6. Let rest for 10 to 20 minutes before serving.

# sheet pan drumsticks and veggie roast

I've said it before, and I'll say it again: Nothing is better than a one-pot or one-sheet pan recipe. Easy cleanup and quick, painless meals. And if it can be healthy as well, all the better. That's my weekday kitchen dream after I've been at the office all day. I do actually love spending hours in the kitchen, but life obviously doesn't allow for that every day, so this recipe is for my modern-day men and women who want something easy and healthy. And my kids love eating chicken drumsticks—they call them "chicken on the bone" because they get a kick out of holding them like a caveman would have!

*Serves 4*

—

¼ cup extra-virgin olive oil

1 teaspoon dried thyme

2 teaspoons salt

½ teaspoon freshly ground
black pepper

1 teaspoon smoked paprika

8 large chicken drumsticks

1 medium red onion, chopped

10 cloves garlic

1 medium sweet potato, diced

1 large parsnip,
peeled and diced

1 bunch carrots,
peeled and diced

1. Preheat the oven to 400°F. Line a large baking sheet with foil.

2. In a small bowl, whisk together the olive oil, thyme, salt, pepper, and paprika.

3. Place the drumsticks, onion, garlic, sweet potato, parsnip, and carrots on the prepared baking sheet. Pour the marinade over the top, tossing to coat the chicken and veggies and making sure to get some marinade under the skin of the drumsticks.

4. Roast the chicken and veggies for 40 to 50 minutes, until the veggies are tender, and the chicken is cooked through.

5. Serve immediately.

# easy butter branzino
## with crispy shallots

Whenever I go out to eat, if branzino is on the menu, I'm ordering it. I love this fish for its light, slightly sweet flavor. Don't let the fact that this recipe uses a whole branzino stop you from making it. I promise it's not as daunting as it might seem, and cooking a whole fish is sure to impress your guests. Branzino is so good—it doesn't take much to knock your socks off (maybe just a little butter!).

*Serves 4*

—

2 (1-pound) whole branzinos

4 cloves garlic, minced

¼ teaspoon salt

⅛ teaspoon freshly ground black pepper

5 tablespoons (⅝ stick) unsalted butter

1 large shallot, thinly sliced

Flaky sea salt

1. Cut the head and tail off the fish if the fishmonger didn't already do it, and cut the bottom of the fish open. Season the fish with the garlic, salt, and pepper, making sure to include the inside.

2. Melt 4 tablespoons of the butter in a large skillet over medium-high heat. Cook the branzino for 6 to 7 minutes, until it starts to flake, then flip the fish and cook another 6 to 7 minutes, or until cooked through. Transfer the branzino to a paper towel–lined plate.

3. Melt the remaining 1 tablespoon butter in the same large skillet. Fry the shallot for 3 to 4 minutes, until golden brown. Transfer the shallot to a paper towel–lined plate to blot the excess oil and sprinkle with flaky sea salt.

4. Carefully separate the fish from the bones by running a fork or spatula between the spine and fish, from the top (where the head was) to the bottom. You can eat the skin if you want!

5. To serve, place a portion of fish on a plate, add crispy shallots on top, and sprinkle with flaky sea salt.

# ten-minute scallops
## with pesto cream

This recipe literally takes about ten minutes, it's so quick. I always have scallops in my freezer and since they're small, they are easy to defrost when you're pinched for time. I'm a pesto junkie, so I usually already have some in my fridge. Or obviously you can use store-bought pesto, which makes this recipe a breeze (but making it fresh is painless and well worth the effort, in my opinion!). This is my go-to when I need something quick and when I need to just throw something together. I love this with Classic Mac-n-Cheese (page 180), since the scallops are so light.

*Serves 2*

—

8 to 12 scallops, depending on how big they are

Salt and freshly ground black pepper

2 tablespoons oat flour

2 tablespoons (¼ stick) unsalted butter

1 tablespoon Pesto (page 254)

1 cup full-fat coconut milk

1. On a large plate, pat the scallops dry with a paper towel, then season them with salt and pepper. Sprinkle them with the flour, then toss to coat. Set aside.

2. Melt the butter in a large skillet over medium heat. Whisk in the pesto and coconut milk. Bring the mixture to a boil, then turn the heat down to medium-low and simmer, whisking occasionally, until slightly thickened, 4 to 5 minutes. Add the scallops and cook for 2 to 3 minutes, until slightly golden brown, then flip the scallops and cook an additional 1 to 2 minutes, until the other side is also slightly golden brown and the scallops are cooked through.

3. Serve the scallops right away with the remaining pesto–coconut milk sauce poured over the top.

# pizza two ways

I had to include my two favorite pizzas in this book and have ranch dressing accompany them. Pizza dipped in ranch reminds me of high school. I would go to Gina's Pizza in Laguna Beach and get the BBQ chicken pizza and smother that baby in ranch. This version is definitely healthier but it still reminds me of the good ole days. Buffalo chicken is another favorite pizza combo of mine, and it is also heaven drenched in ranch dressing.

---

## buffalo chicken pizza

*Serves 2 to 4*

—

1 store-bought pizza crust (I like Cappello's Naked Pizza Crust)

2 Perfectly Cooked Chicken Thighs (page 248), shredded

½ cup plus 3 tablespoons of your favorite buffalo sauce

½ cup grated Manchego cheese

4 ounces soft goat's-milk cheese

1½ tablespoons chopped fresh chives

Ranch Dressing (page 264), for serving

1. Cook the pizza crust according to the directions on the package (until it's time to put the toppings on). Leave the oven on and turn to 400°F.

2. Place the chicken in a medium bowl, add 3 tablespoons of the buffalo sauce, and mix well.

3. Place the remaining ½ cup buffalo sauce on top of the pizza crust, spreading it out up to the edges to lightly cover the crust. Sprinkle the Manchego around the crust, followed by the chicken. Using your fingers, place pieces of goat's-milk cheese on top.

4. Bake for 10 to 15 minutes until the cheese is melted.

5. To serve, top the pizza with chives and drizzle with ranch dressing.

# bbq chicken pizza

*Serves 2 to 4*

—

1 store-bought pizza crust
(I like Cappello's Naked
Pizza Crust)

2 Perfectly Cooked Chicken
Thighs (page 248), shredded

½ cup plus 3 tablespoons of
your favorite BBQ sauce

1 teaspoon avocado oil

½ small red onion, thinly sliced

½ cup grated Manchego
cheese

4 ounces soft goat's-milk
cheese

Ranch Dressing (page 264),
for serving

1. Cook the pizza crust according to the directions on the package (until it's time to put the toppings on). Leave the oven on and turn to 400°F.

2. Place the chicken in a medium bowl, add 3 tablespoons of the BBQ sauce, and mix well.

3. Warm the avocado oil in a medium skillet over medium heat. Add the onion and cook until soft, 5 to 6 minutes.

4. Place the remaining ½ cup BBQ sauce on top of the pizza crust, spreading it out up to the edges to lightly cover the crust. Spread the Manchego around the crust, followed by the chicken. Using your fingers, place pieces of goat's-milk cheese on top, followed by the onion.

5. Bake for 10 to 15 minutes until the cheese is melted.

6. To serve, drizzle ranch dressing on the pizza.

# mediterranean meatballs
## with tzatziki sauce

These meatballs have a strong cumin flavor and remind me of being in Greece (which, by far, has the best food on the planet!). Out of everywhere I've traveled, that's been my favorite country, because everything is so fresh and clean, which makes the food so flavorful. Plus, you can find tzatziki sauce on every menu. I like serving this with the Gluten-Free Naan (see page 207).

---

*Makes 35 meatballs*

—

1 medium yellow onion, coarsely chopped

2 pounds ground beef

6 cloves garlic, minced

1 teaspoon freshly ground black pepper

2 teaspoons salt

2 teaspoons ground cumin

2 teaspoons dried oregano

1 teaspoon ground cinnamon

2 large eggs

½ cup panko breadcrumbs

Tzatziki Sauce (page 251)

1. Preheat the oven to 400°F. Line a large baking sheet with parchment paper.

2. Place the onion in a food processor and pulse until it resembles mush. In a large bowl, combine well the beef, garlic, pepper, salt, cumin, oregano, cinnamon, eggs, and breadcrumbs (I like using my hands). Roll the beef mixture into portions the size of golf balls. Place the meatballs on the prepared baking sheet.

3. Bake for 25 to 30 minutes, until cooked through. Serve the meatballs with Tzatziki Sauce.

# sides

# charred green beans
## with tonnato

Tonnato is an Italian sauce made with tuna that is so, so yummy. It's whipped up so it's smooth and creamy and more of a tuna mayo than anything. I love it with the charred green beans here, but it would also be good with meat (pork or beef). In addition to being perfect as a side for a dinner, this could be a nice lunch.

---

*Serves 4 to 6*

—

2 tablespoons avocado oil

2 pounds green beans

Salt

2 small oil-packed anchovies

½ cup mayo

3 tablespoons lime juice (from about 2 limes)

Freshly ground black pepper

¼ cup extra-virgin olive oil, plus more for drizzling

½ jalapeño, seeds removed, chopped

1 (6.7-ounce) can oil-packed tuna, drained

1. Heat the avocado oil in a large skillet over high heat. Add the green beans and a pinch of salt. Let the green beans cook, without stirring, until they're charred, about 5 minutes. Flip and cook an additional 2 to 3 minutes, until charred.

2. Place the anchovies, mayo, lime juice, a pinch of pepper, the olive oil, jalapeño, tuna, 1 teaspoon salt, and 2 tablespoons water in a high-powered blender. Blend on high until smooth, about 30 seconds.

3. To serve, spread the tonnato on the bottom of a large serving plate. Place the green beans on top and drizzle with a little olive oil.

# sweet harissa cauliflower

This recipe was inspired by a dish at True Food Kitchen, which is one of my favorite quick and healthy restaurants here in Nashville (they have other locations as well). Their spicy cauliflower paired with the sweetness of the dates was a combination I never knew I needed. I've been known to make this recipe regularly for lunch, because I just love it so much and I could honestly eat it almost every day. I also like serving this with the New York Strip Steak (page 160) and the Grilled Lamb Skewers (page 139).

*Serves 4*

—

1 medium head cauliflower, cut into florets

1 tablespoon extra-virgin olive oil

Salt and freshly ground black pepper

3 large dates, pitted and chopped

1½ teaspoons chopped fresh dill

½ teaspoon chopped fresh mint

—

**tahini-harissa sauce**

3 tablespoons tahini

3 tablespoons harissa

¼ teaspoon garlic powder

1 tablespoon fresh lemon juice

1 tablespoon pure maple syrup

Salt and freshly ground black pepper

1. Preheat the oven to 400°F. Line a large baking sheet with parchment paper.

2. Place the cauliflower on the prepared baking sheet. Coat with the olive oil and season with salt and pepper. Roast the cauliflower until it is tender, 25 to 30 minutes. Then broil it for 2 minutes, until slightly charred.

3. Meanwhile, make the tahini-harissa sauce: In a medium bowl, whisk together the tahini, harissa, garlic powder, lemon juice, and maple syrup. Season with salt and pepper and stir.

4. Place the cauliflower in a large bowl. Pour the sauce on top and toss to coat.

5. To serve, place the cauliflower on a large serving platter. Sprinkle the dates, dill, and mint on top.

# roasted broccoli
## with anchovy breadcrumbs

If you haven't cooked with anchovies yet, please trust me and give them a try. They offer a perfect salty, umami flavor to the dish and aren't overpowering, I promise. Plus, the anchovy breadcrumbs give this broccoli a nice little crunch. I make broccoli at least three times a week, so this is a nice departure from my ordinary roasted broccoli.

*Serves 4*

—

1 large head broccoli, cut into bite-size pieces

3 tablespoons plus 2 teaspoons extra-virgin olive oil, plus more for serving

Salt and freshly ground black pepper

3 (½-inch-thick) slices sourdough bread, crust removed and coarsely chopped (about 1½ cups)

1 (2-ounce) can oil-packed anchovy fillets

1 large clove garlic, minced

½ teaspoon red pepper flakes

1. Preheat the oven to 400°F. Line a large baking sheet with parchment paper.

2. Place the broccoli on the prepared baking sheet. Drizzle with 3 tablespoons of the olive oil and season with salt and pepper. Roast the broccoli for 30 minutes, until it is slightly charred.

3. Meanwhile, make the breadcrumbs: Place the bread in a food processor. Pulse until you have coarse crumbs. Set aside.

4. Place a large skillet over medium heat. Drain 1 teaspoon of the oil from the anchovies and place it in the skillet. Add the remaining 2 teaspoons olive oil and the anchovies and cook for 1 minute, until the anchovies dissolve. Add the garlic and cook until it is aromatic, about 30 seconds.

5. Turn the heat to medium-high and add the breadcrumbs and red pepper flakes. Cook for 3 to 5 minutes, until the breadcrumbs are toasted.

6. To serve, place the broccoli on a serving plate. Sprinkle with breadcrumbs and drizzle with olive oil. Serve immediately.

# roasted eggplant
## with tahini drizzle

This recipe is all about the tahini dressing—it's salty and sweet and would be good on just about any roasted veggie. I used roasted eggplant here because I love it, and I think eggplant is underused. It's full of fiber and contains vitamins A and C, which are antioxidants, making it really good for you.

---

*Serves 4*

—

1 large eggplant, thinly sliced crosswise

3 tablespoons extra-virgin olive oil

Salt and freshly ground black pepper

—

**tahini drizzle**

3 tablespoons extra-virgin olive oil

1 tablespoon pure maple syrup

2 tablespoons tamari

2 tablespoons tahini

1 clove garlic, coarsely chopped

1. Preheat the oven to 400°F. Line a large baking sheet with parchment paper.

2. Place the eggplant on the prepared baking sheet. Coat with the olive oil and season with salt and pepper. Roast the eggplant for 18 to 20 minutes, until it is golden brown and tender.

3. Meanwhile, make the tahini drizzle: Place the olive oil, maple syrup, tamari, tahini, garlic, and 2 tablespoons water in a high-powered blender. Blend on high until smooth.

4. To serve, place the eggplant on a large serving platter and spoon the tahini drizzle on top.

# brown butter asparagus

My kids have their favorite veggies, and asparagus is one of them. Since I make it often, I'm always trying to think of new ways to keep them interested. This is my current favorite: asparagus in brown butter with crispy garlic and shaved Manchego cheese. Need I say more?

---

*Serves 4*

—

1 bunch asparagus

Extra-virgin olive oil, for drizzling

Salt and freshly ground black pepper

¼ cup (½ stick) unsalted butter

2 cloves garlic, minced, plus 8 large cloves, thinly sliced

1 tablespoon fresh lemon juice

1 tablespoon avocado oil

2 tablespoons shaved Manchego cheese

1. Preheat the oven to 425°F. Line a large baking sheet with parchment paper.

2. Place the asparagus on the prepared baking sheet in a single layer. Drizzle with a little olive oil and season with salt and pepper. Roast the asparagus until it is crisp-tender, about 10 minutes.

3. Meanwhile, in a small saucepan, cook the butter over medium-high heat, stirring occasionally, until it froths and starts to brown, about 3 minutes. Add the minced garlic and cook, whisking consistently, until it is aromatic, about 30 seconds. Remove the saucepan from the heat.

4. Add the lemon juice to the butter and stir to combine. Pour the brown butter into a small bowl and set aside.

5. In the same saucepan, warm the avocado oil over medium-high heat. Add the sliced garlic and cook, stirring often, until it is golden brown, 2 to 3 minutes. Transfer the garlic to a paper towel–lined plate.

6. To serve, place the asparagus on a serving plate. Pour the brown butter on top and sprinkle with the crispy garlic and shaved Manchego.

# mac-n-cheese
# two ways

Lord, help me. This recipe is *insanely good*. The cheese sauce is next level. It's exactly what you want from mac-n-cheese—creamy, velvety heaven. Jaxon asks for the classic version all the time, and I usually make the pesto version for myself. I justify it's not that bad since I'm still getting in some greens with the spinach and pesto . . . Whatever we need to tell ourselves, right?

## classic mac-n-cheese

*Serves 4*

—

1 (8-ounce) package elbow pasta

1 cup grated Manchego cheese

2 cups grated white cheddar cheese

½ cup (1 stick) unsalted butter

½ cup oat flour

2 cups oat milk

½ teaspoon salt

½ teaspoon freshly ground black pepper

¼ teaspoon paprika

1. Cook the pasta according to the directions on the package, then drain and rinse (to prevent sticking).

2. In a large bowl, toss the Manchego and cheddar together to combine. Set aside.

3. In a large saucepan, melt the butter over medium heat. Add the flour and whisk for about 1 minute, until it resembles wet sand. Add the oat milk, stirring constantly, until the sauce is smooth and has thickened, 4 to 5 minutes. Remove the saucepan from the heat. Stir in the salt, pepper, and paprika. Add the cheese and stir to combine until smooth.

4. Add the pasta to the cheese mixture and mix well.

5. Serve immediately.

# creamy pesto spinach mac-n-cheese

*Serves 4*

—

1 (8-ounce) package elbow pasta

1 cup grated Manchego cheese

2 cups grated white cheddar cheese

3 tablespoons Pesto (page 254)

½ cup (1 stick) unsalted butter

½ cup oat flour

2 cups oat milk

1 cup chopped spinach

½ teaspoon salt

½ teaspoon freshly ground black pepper

¼ teaspoon paprika

1. Cook the pasta according to the directions on the package, then drain and rinse (to prevent sticking).

2. In a large bowl, toss the Manchego and cheddar together with the pesto to combine. Set aside.

3. In a large saucepan, melt the butter over medium heat. Add the flour and whisk for about 1 minute, until it resembles wet sand. Add the oat milk and spinach, stirring constantly, until the sauce is smooth and has thickened and the spinach has wilted, 4 to 5 minutes. Remove the saucepan from the heat. Stir in the salt, pepper, and paprika. Add the cheese and stir to combine until smooth.

4. Add the pasta to the cheese mixture and mix well.

5. Serve immediately.

# garlic okra

A few years ago, I didn't even know what okra was. Now I love it for its sweet but earthy flavor and get it at the farmers market every weekend during the summer months. Okra's flavors can change, depending on how you cook it. It can be crispy and juicy or dense and creamy. It is packed with tons of vitamins like C, K, and A, and it is loaded with magnesium, antioxidants, and fiber. Plus, this recipe takes only about ten minutes. So, what are you waiting for?

---

*Serves 4*

—

½ cup avocado oil

2 large shallots, thinly sliced

4 cloves garlic, minced

1 pound okra, halved lengthwise

Salt and freshly ground black pepper

1. Heat the avocado oil in a large skillet over medium-high heat. Add the shallots and garlic and sauté until the garlic is aromatic and the shallots are tender, about 3 minutes. Add the okra and cook until it is tender and slightly golden brown, 8 to 10 minutes. Season with salt and pepper.

2. Serve warm.

# gluten-free cheddar buns

When I was creating the recipes for this book, this is the one that gave me the hardest time. I actually almost scrapped it. But then I told myself to just give it one more go, and luckily, that time was the winner. I made a few batches that were amazing right out of the oven—but a day or two later they were super dense. That's when I knew I had to abandon the oat flour (oat flour is normally my go-to for baking). My kids are obsessed with biscuits, so I'm glad I stayed the course and perfected this for them. Gluten-free baking can offer up challenges, but I've found that almond flour really is one of the best options. Plus, the cheese in these helps bring in moisture. If you've ever been to Red Lobster (yes, I went often growing up), these remind me of their cheddar biscuits. But in my true fashion, these are much healthier.

---

*Makes 12*

—

2½ cups almond flour

1 tablespoon coconut sugar

1 tablespoon baking powder

½ teaspoon salt

1½ teaspoons garlic powder

1 teaspoon onion powder

½ cup virgin coconut oil, melted

½ cup full-fat coconut milk

½ cup plain yogurt

1 large egg

2 cups shredded cheddar cheese

Salted butter, for serving

1. Preheat the oven to 450°F. Line a large baking sheet with parchment paper.

2. In a large bowl, combine the flour, coconut sugar, baking powder, salt, garlic powder, and onion powder.

3. In another large bowl, whisk together the coconut oil, coconut milk, yogurt, and egg. Add the wet ingredients to the dry ingredients and mix to combine. Fold in the cheddar.

4. Spoon the batter onto the prepared baking sheet, about ¼ cup per biscuit.

5. Bake for 12 minutes, until golden brown.

6. The buns are best served warm with a little butter.

# miso scallion noodles

Sometimes I dream about these noodles because I love them so much. They're super creamy (but without dairy) and they have buckwheat soba noodles, which are gluten-free and still delicious. My daughter, Saylor, could eat these every single day.

---

*Serves 4*

—

10 scallions

¾ cup avocado oil

1 (8-ounce) package buckwheat soba noodles

2 tablespoons white miso paste

2 tablespoons tamari

1. Cut the scallions crosswise into thirds, separating the dark green part from the white part and the pale green part. Slice the dark green and white parts lengthwise into very thin strips, keeping the two parts separate.

2. Pour the avocado oil into a large skillet over medium-low heat. Add the white part of the scallions and cook for 5 minutes, until slightly golden brown. Add the dark green part of the scallions and cook until it's crispy and a deep golden brown, about 20 minutes. Using a slotted spoon, transfer the scallions to a paper towel–lined plate to blot the excess oil.

3. Chop the light green part of the scallions. Add it to the same large skillet and sauté until it's golden brown, about 5 minutes. Pour the scallion oil through a fine-mesh sieve into a bowl and discard any solids.

4. Cook the noodles according to the directions on the package with 1 tablespoon of the scallion oil. Drain the noodles and rinse (to prevent sticking). Return the noodles to the pot that they were cooked in. Add ½ cup of the scallion oil, tossing to combine.

5. In a small bowl, whisk together the miso and tamari until combined. Add this mixture to the noodles and toss to combine.

6. To serve, scoop the noodles into a bowl, then break up the crispy scallions and sprinkle them on top.

# bacon-wrapped asparagus

Bacon is really the only pork we eat in my family. But we do eat it regularly, since my boys really love it. These bacon-wrapped asparagus are a great side (especially for kids) because they offer the perfect salty crunch to so many recipes. They also make a great finger-food app at a party.

---

*Serves 4*

—

1 (12-ounce) package bacon, cut in half

1 bunch asparagus

Extra-virgin olive oil, for drizzling

Salt and freshly ground black pepper

1. Preheat the oven 400°F. Line a large baking sheet with parchment paper.

2. Take one piece of bacon and, starting at the bottom of the asparagus stalk, slowly wrap the bacon all the way up. Place on the prepared baking sheet. Repeat with the remaining asparagus stalks and bacon slices.

3. Drizzle the bacon-wrapped asparagus with olive oil and season with salt and pepper.

4. Bake for 30 to 35 minutes, until the bacon is golden brown.

# zucchini butter pasta

Butter pasta is a favorite comfort food in my house (I honestly like it as much as my kids do). I always love adding veggies to a dish for the extra health boost, especially when you either can't taste them (this is more for my kids) or when they just add another dimension of flavor. In this recipe, the zucchini is grated, so it gets mushy and buttery and becomes part of the sauce.

---

*Serves 2 to 4*

—

1 (8-ounce) package spaghetti

2 medium zucchini, grated (about 2 cups)

6 tablespoons (¾ stick) unsalted butter

4 cloves garlic, minced

1 teaspoon salt

½ teaspoon red pepper flakes

½ cup grated Manchego cheese

2 tablespoons chopped fresh basil

1. Cook the spaghetti according to the directions on the package, but stop 1 minute before it's fully cooked. Reserve ¼ cup of the pasta water. Drain the noodles and set them aside.

2. Place the grated zucchini in a nut bag or dish towel. Squeeze out the extra moisture over the sink.

3. In a large saucepan, melt the butter over medium-high heat. Add the garlic and cook until it is fragrant, about 30 seconds. Add the zucchini, salt, and red pepper flakes and bring to a simmer. Cook the zucchini for 12 minutes, stirring occasionally, until it has thickened and is a sauce-like consistency. Remove the saucepan from the heat.

4. Add the pasta water to the sauce and stir to combine. Then add the spaghetti and ¼ cup of the Manchego and stir to combine.

5. To serve, divide the pasta mixture between the bowls and top with the remaining Manchego and the basil.

# smashed purple sweet potatoes

Sweet potatoes have the perfect amount of sweetness and don't take much since they're already so good on their own. They're also loaded with vitamins and beta-carotene. In this recipe, I leave the onions off for two of my three kids—only my oldest will go near them. Make these with Sweet Balsamic Chicken Thighs (page 152) or Easy Butter Branzino with Crispy Shallots (page 163).

*Makes 8*

—

8 very small purple sweet potatoes

Extra-virgin olive oil, for drizzling

Salt and freshly ground black pepper

2 tablespoons (¼ stick) unsalted butter, melted

½ cup grated Manchego cheese

4 small scallions, white and green parts, thinly sliced

1. Preheat the oven to 425°F. Line a large baking sheet with foil.

2. Place the sweet potatoes on the prepared baking sheet, then drizzle with olive oil and season with salt and pepper. Bake for 35 to 40 minutes, until fork-tender.

3. Flatten the potatoes by pressing down on them with the back of a fork. Drizzle the potatoes with the butter and season with salt and pepper. Bake for 30 to 35 minutes, or until crispy.

4. Sprinkle the potatoes with the Manchego, then bake for another 2 to 3 minutes, until the cheese is melted.

5. Top with the scallions and serve.

# sour cream and chive potato salad with crispy shallots

For years, I didn't eat sour cream because I was staying away from cow's milk. But now it's back in my life. I've actually found that I'm able to tolerate sour cream (and butter, yay) and my kids do as well. In fact, a lot of people with casein sensitivities can tolerate both sour cream and butter because of the fermentation process for these ingredients. How great is that?!

---

*Serves 6*

—

1½ pounds red potatoes or rainbow fingerling potatoes

Extra-virgin olive oil, for coating

Salt and freshly ground black pepper

2 teaspoons Dijon mustard

2 tablespoons white wine vinegar

1 medium shallot, finely chopped (about ¼ cup)

3 tablespoons avocado oil

1 large shallot, thinly sliced (about ½ cup)

3 tablespoons mayo

2 tablespoons sour cream

1 tablespoon fresh lemon juice

½ teaspoon garlic powder

2 scallions, white and green parts, finely sliced

¼ cup chopped fresh chives

1. Preheat the oven to 425°F. Line a large baking sheet with foil.

2. Place the potatoes on the prepared baking sheet. Coat with the olive oil, then season with salt and pepper. Roast the potatoes for 25 minutes, until they are fork-tender.

3. In a large bowl, whisk together the mustard, vinegar, chopped shallot, a big pinch of salt, and a pinch of pepper.

4. Quarter the potatoes, place them in the bowl with the dressing, and toss to coat. Let the potatoes cool completely in the fridge, about 1 hour.

5. Meanwhile, warm the avocado oil in a large skillet over medium-high heat. Add the sliced shallot and fry until it is golden brown, about 5 minutes. Transfer the shallot to a paper towel–lined plate to blot the excess oil and sprinkle with a pinch of salt. Set aside.

6. In a small bowl, combine the mayo, sour cream, lemon juice, and garlic powder. Pour the dressing on the potatoes. Add the scallions and chives and stir to incorporate.

7. To serve, sprinkle the crispy shallots on top of the potato salad.

# classic bbq coleslaw

The only reason coleslaw has gotten a bad rep in the past is because it's heavy in mayo, which when made with soybean or canola oil causes inflammation in the body. I use Primal Kitchen's avocado mayo, which is made with avocado oil. So, I would actually say this coleslaw is healthy and I gobble it up. The touch of sugar gives it that extra pop of flavor and helps bring everything together. I like making this when I'm hosting a big group during the summer. Serve it with all the traditional BBQ staples: chicken wings, baked beans, Gluten-Free Honey Cornbread (page 198), and Sour Cream and Chive Potato Salad with Crispy Shallots (page 192).

*Serves 6*

—

1 medium head green cabbage

3 medium carrots, grated

1 cup mayo

¼ cup sour cream

2 tablespoons finely chopped leeks

2 tablespoons raw cane sugar

1 tablespoon white wine vinegar

1 tablespoon Dijon mustard

Salt and freshly ground black pepper

1. Quarter the cabbage through the core, then cut out the core. Cut each quarter in half crosswise, then finely shred. Place the shredded cabbage in a large bowl. Add the carrots.

2. In a medium bowl, combine the mayo, sour cream, leeks, sugar, vinegar, and mustard. Season with salt and pepper.

3. Pour the dressing over the cabbage mixture and toss to combine.

4. Serve immediately or chill for up to 8 hours.

# cucumber sunomono salad

This Japanese dish is light and refreshing and makes a great side, but it could also be used on top of fish as a garnish. I sometimes just eat a whole bowl of this salad for lunch. The key is to use a mandoline to slice the cucumbers so they're super thin. This recipe makes extra dressing that you can use on a salad later in the week. I like serving this side with Nobu's Black Cod (page 148) and Miso Scallion Noodles (page 186).

---

*Serves 2*

—

1 large English cucumber or 4 Persian cucumbers, thinly sliced on a mandoline

½ teaspoon salt

—

**sweet vinegar dressing**

3 tablespoons rice vinegar

1 tablespoon pure maple syrup

¼ teaspoon salt

¼ teaspoon tamari

1 teaspoon toasted sesame seeds

1. Place the sliced cucumbers in a medium colander. Sprinkle with the salt and toss with your hands to coat. Let the cucumbers sit for 10 minutes to draw out excess moisture. Squeeze the cucumbers to remove excess moisture, then transfer them to a medium bowl (your hands are the best tool here).

2. Meanwhile, make the sweet vinegar dressing: In a medium bowl, whisk together the vinegar, maple syrup, salt, tamari, and sesame seeds.

3. Pour 2 tablespoons of the dressing on the cucumbers and toss to coat. Add more dressing, if desired.

4. The extra dressing will keep well in an airtight container in the fridge for up to 10 days.

# roasted carrots
## with manchego

Carrots are loaded with beta-carotene and vitamin A, plus they have a ton of fiber. Since they're a touch sweet, I have no issues getting my kids to eat these. You can swap Parmesan for the Manchego, if desired. I make these with Air Fryer Chicken Nuggets with Chick-fil-A–Inspired Sauce (page 112) and Classic Mac-n-Cheese (page 180) for a kid-friendly meal.

*Serves 6*

—

2 pounds rainbow carrots, peeled

2 tablespoons extra-virgin olive oil

2 small cloves garlic, minced

1 teaspoon salt

½ cup grated Manchego cheese

1. Preheat the oven to 400°F. Line a large baking sheet with parchment paper.

2. Place the carrots on the prepared baking sheet.

3. In a small bowl, combine the olive oil, garlic, and salt. Pour the oil mixture over the carrots and toss to combine.

4. Roast the carrots until they are fork-tender, 25 to 30 minutes. Sprinkle Manchego on the carrots, then bake another 4 to 5 minutes, until the cheese is golden brown.

# gluten-free honey cornbread

I first made this to bring to a friend's house on Halloween. She was making the chili, so I brought the cornbread. My kids went crazy for it, probably because the honey gives it just the right amount of sweetness. Cornbread is something I like to make year-round. Yes, Halloween with chili was amazing, but I also like it at a summer BBQ with my Classic BBQ Coleslaw (page 193).

*Serves 6 to 8*

—

⅓ cup virgin coconut oil, melted, plus more for the pan

1 cup cornmeal

1 cup all-purpose gluten-free flour

1 tablespoon baking powder

1 teaspoon salt

½ cup raw honey

1 cup full-fat coconut milk

1 large egg

1. Preheat the oven to 400°F. Grease an 8 × 8-inch baking dish with coconut oil.

2. In a large bowl, combine the cornmeal, flour, baking powder, and salt.

3. In a medium bowl, whisk together the honey, coconut milk, coconut oil, and egg until combined. Pour the wet ingredients into the dry ingredients and mix well.

4. Pour the batter into the prepared baking dish and bake for 25 to 30 minutes, until a toothpick comes out clean and the top is golden brown.

# snacks

---

# gluten-free pbj oat bars
## with raspberry sauce

I came up with this recipe specifically for my oldest, Cam. He's my peanut-butter-and-jelly guy. I love having bars on hand for quick snacks for the kiddos—especially ones that I know are healthy, with no hidden additives. When it comes to peanut butter, look for a brand that contains only peanuts and a little bit of salt. No added sugar or inflammation-causing oils.

---

*Makes 16*

—

**raspberry sauce**

1½ cups raspberries

Juice of 1 lemon
(about 2 tablespoons)

¼ cup coconut sugar

1 tablespoon oat flour

—

**peanut butter base**

¼ cup (½ stick) unsalted
butter

¼ cup pure maple syrup

½ cup crunchy peanut butter

½ cup oat flour

1 cup gluten-free rolled oats

1. Preheat the oven to 375°F. Line a 9 × 9-inch baking dish with parchment paper.

2. Make the raspberry sauce: In a small saucepan, combine the raspberries, lemon juice, and coconut sugar and cook over medium-high heat until it is mostly liquid and the raspberries are mush, about 4 minutes. Add the oat flour and stir to combine. Remove the saucepan from the heat.

3. Make the peanut butter base: In another small saucepan, melt the butter over medium heat. Add the maple syrup and peanut butter and stir until combined. Remove the saucepan from the heat.

4. Place the oat flour and oats in a large bowl. Add the peanut butter mixture and stir well. Drizzle the raspberry sauce on top of the peanut butter base, folding a few times but not mixing completely.

5. Press the mixture into the prepared baking dish. Bake for 25 to 28 minutes, until the edges are browned. Cool in the pan for 10 minutes before placing on a wire rack to cool completely. Cut into bars to serve.

# pimento cheese dip

I had never heard of pimento cheese before I moved to Tennessee. I first had it when I went to Blackberry Farm (the most magical getaway on a farm here in Tennessee—worth looking up if you've never heard of it) and instantly became a fan. Traditional pimento cheese uses regular cheddar cheese, but I've swapped that for goat's-milk cheese, since we limit the cow products we consume. You can eat this right away, but it's better if you can let it chill in the fridge for thirty minutes or so.

---

*Serves 4*

—

½ cup soft goat's-milk cheese

1½ cups grated goat's-milk cheddar cheese

4 ounces pimientos, drained

1 teaspoon onion powder

¼ teaspoon garlic powder

½ teaspoon cayenne pepper

½ teaspoon salt

½ jalapeño, seeds removed, finely chopped

½ cup mayo

1. In a medium bowl, combine both cheeses, the pimientos, onion powder, garlic powder, cayenne, salt, jalapeño, and mayo. Enjoy right away or let chill in the fridge for 30 minutes.

2. The dip will keep well in an airtight container in the fridge for up to 7 days.

# tuna poke

Tuna poke is an ideal summer lunch, snack, or appetizer because it's light and refreshing but has so much flavor. I use coconut aminos instead of soy sauce because it's healthier (it's soy-, gluten-, and dairy-free) and it has a slightly sweeter flavor. Make sure to get sushi-grade ahi tuna for the best, freshest flavor.

---

*Serves 4*

—

1 pound ahi tuna, chopped

2 Persian cucumbers, chopped

½ small yellow onion, finely chopped

4 scallions, white part only, finely chopped

1 jalapeño, seeds removed, finely chopped

Toasted sesame seeds, for garnish

—

**dressing**

¼ cup coconut aminos

Juice of 1 lime (about 2 tablespoons)

½ teaspoon grated fresh ginger

1 tablespoon toasted sesame oil

½ teaspoon toasted sesame seeds

1. In a large bowl, combine the tuna, cucumbers, onion, scallion, and jalapeño.

2. Make the dressing: In a small bowl, whisk together the aminos, lime juice, ginger, sesame oil, and sesame seeds.

3. Pour the dressing on the tuna mixture and stir to combine. Let sit in the fridge for 20 to 30 minutes for the flavors to combine.

4. To serve, top with more sesame seeds.

# gluten-free naan
## with tzatziki sauce

Naan is a fried flatbread made with yogurt, which gives it a soft texture. Serve this with Mediterranean Meatballs (page 169) or Grilled Lamb Skewers (page 139) to feel like you're in the Mediterranean having a beautiful dinner. A bottle of wine is also welcome.

---

*Makes 7*

—

¼ cup plain yogurt

½ cup full-fat coconut milk, plus more as needed

1 teaspoon extra-virgin olive oil

2 teaspoons baking powder

½ teaspoon salt

2 small cloves garlic, minced

½ cup coconut flour, plus more as needed

½ cup arrowroot powder

½ cup tapioca flour

Avocado oil, for the pan

Tzatziki Sauce (page 251), for dipping

1. In a medium bowl, whisk together the yogurt, coconut milk, olive oil, baking powder, salt, and garlic. Add the coconut flour, arrowroot powder, and tapioca flour. Mix until you have a doughlike consistency that's moist but not sticky. If it's too sticky, just add a little more coconut flour, and if it's too dry, just add a little more coconut milk.

2. Dust the workstation with coconut flour. Take a small handful of dough and place it in the middle of the floured surface. Sprinkle a little more coconut flour on top, then roll it out until it's about ¼ inch thick. Repeat with the remaining dough.

3. Heat a large skillet over medium-high heat. Coat with avocado oil. Fry the dough for 2 to 3 minutes, until golden brown. Using a metal spatula, carefully flip the dough and fry the other side for an additional 1 to 2 minutes, until it is also golden brown. Transfer the naan to a parchment-lined plate. Repeat with the remaining dough. When each piece is done frying, cover it with another piece of parchment to keep it warm and to separate it from the other pieces.

4. Serve the naan with tzatziki sauce, for dipping.

# baked goat's-milk cheese and tomato dip

This is a good dish to make when you need to bring an app to a friend's house for dinner. I've found it's always a hit with a big group of people. It's really good warm, but I actually like it better cold! When making it for the first time, plan on serving it warm, and store any leftovers in the fridge. Then give it a try when it's cold, so you can see which way you like it better. It's thicker cold, which is why I like it.

---

*Serves 6*

—

8 ounces soft goat's-milk cheese

1 cup grated Manchego cheese

½ cup mayo

1 medium yellow onion, finely chopped

½ teaspoon freshly ground black pepper

Salt

1 cup cherry tomatoes, halved

¼ cup panko breadcrumbs

10 fresh basil leaves, julienned (optional)

1 (32-ounce) bag tortilla chips, for serving

1. Preheat the oven to 375°F.

2. In a medium bowl, combine the goat's-milk cheese, Manchego, mayo, onion, pepper, and a pinch of salt. Place in an 8 × 8-inch baking dish. Lay the tomatoes on top.

3. Bake for 45 to 50 minutes, or until the edges are browning and the tomatoes are slightly roasted. Remove the baking dish from the oven and turn the broiler on. Sprinkle the breadcrumbs on top. Broil for 1 to 3 minutes, until browned and bubbling. Garnish with basil, if using.

4. Let cool 10 minutes before serving.

5. Serve with tortilla chips, for dipping.

# spicy grilled peaches
## with balsamic glaze

I get so excited when I first see the peach truck pull up at the farmers market come springtime. Then I know the summer months are close, which means lots of grilling for my household. I've become a decent griller in the past two years, so I'm always coming up with new food to grill. If you've never had a grilled peach, you're in for a real treat. They taste ever-so-smoky with the center maintaining its perfect, juicy sweetness. I could drizzle balsamic glaze on just about anything, but the tartness is heaven with the sweetness of the peaches. This is also a great app at a BBQ.

*Serves 6*

—

Avocado oil, for the grill or grill pan

4 peaches, pitted, each cut into 8 wedges

2 medium hothouse tomatoes or 1 large heirloom tomato, cut into 8 wedges

3 tablespoons your favorite store-bought balsamic glaze

¼ teaspoon cayenne pepper

1 teaspoon rosemary, finely chopped

Flaky sea salt

1. Heat a grill or grill pan over medium-high heat. Coat the grill with avocado oil. Grill the peaches on one side for 6 to 8 minutes, until slightly charred. Flip the peaches and cook for another 4 to 5 minutes, until slightly charred. Remove the peaches from the heat.

2. To serve, place the peaches on a serving plate. Arrange the tomatoes in between the peaches. Drizzle the balsamic glaze over the top and sprinkle the fruit with the cayenne pepper and rosemary. Garnish with a pinch of flaky sea salt.

# cashew butter espresso bites

I love snacks that are quick and easy, especially if I'm at the office, running around with the kids, or traveling. I always have a snack on me, no matter what, and these are healthy, easy to throw in your purse, and give you a little energy boost. Just be careful your kids don't get ahold of these! Mine have eaten them—and they loved them—but coffee is the *last* thing they need!

---

*Makes 14*

—

1 cup cashew butter

¼ cup coconut flour

1 tablespoon instant coffee

2 teaspoons pure maple syrup

1 tablespoon hemp seeds

1. Line a large baking sheet with parchment paper.

2. In a medium bowl, combine the cashew butter, coconut flour, coffee, maple syrup, and hemp seeds. Roll the dough into 14 golf ball–size balls and place them on the prepared baking sheet.

3. Place the baking sheet in the fridge until the bites harden, about 30 minutes. Enjoy right away or store in a zip-top bag in the fridge.

4. The espresso bites will keep well in the fridge for up to 14 days.

# bacon-wrapped goat's-milk cheese–stuffed dates

Anything is good wrapped in bacon, but add dates and goat's-milk cheese and it's an explosion of flavor in your mouth in the best way possible. You get salty and sweet in every bite. These are great as an app at a party or as a snack when the kids have friends over. Or if you just want something really decadent and delicious. In a nutshell, there's never a bad time for these bad boys.

---

*Makes 12*

—

12 large dates, pitted

6 teaspoons soft goat's-milk cheese

6 slices bacon, cut in half

1 teaspoon ground cinnamon

1. Preheat the oven to 425°F. Line a medium baking sheet with parchment paper.

2. Cut off the ends of the dates and remove the pits by slightly pulling them apart without separating them.

3. Stuff each date with ½ teaspoon of the goat's-milk cheese, then wrap each date in a piece of bacon, securing it with a toothpick. Place the bacon-wrapped dates on the prepared baking sheet and sprinkle cinnamon on top.

4. Bake for 10 to 15 minutes, until the bacon starts to crisp.

5. Let cool 10 minutes before serving.

6. The dates will keep well in the fridge for up to 4 days (if you can get them to last that long).

# whipped feta
## with figs and honey

At the time of writing this cookbook, whipped feta was having a real moment. I was ordering it every time I saw it on the menu when I went out to eat. I honestly couldn't believe how insanely good it was the first few times I had it. Then I finally decided to look up a recipe to see what the heck was in it that was making it so good. And there it was: *cream cheese*. No wonder it's so insanely good! And that's when I decided a little cream cheese here and there won't kill ya. This is *worth it*! If you can't find figs, this whipped feta is also good with raspberries or sliced strawberries.

*Serves 4*

—

5 ounces feta, broken into chunks

4 ounces cream cheese, at room temperature

1 tablespoon plain yogurt

Salt and freshly ground black pepper

6 large or 8 small Mission figs, halved

2 tablespoons raw honey

4 sprigs thyme, chopped

Flaky sea salt

1. Place the feta, cream cheese, and yogurt in the bowl of a stand mixer, then beat on high until light and fluffy, about 30 seconds. Season with salt and pepper.

2. To serve, spread the feta mixture on a small plate (you want the mixture to be semi-thick). Place the figs and drizzle the honey on top, then sprinkle with the thyme and flaky sea salt.

# panfried shishito peppers
## with spicy garlic aioli

Shishito peppers are a yummy, healthy, crowd-pleasing finger food. But be careful with these peppers—because while most of them are mild, in every ten peppers there's one that'll knock your socks off with heat! I love that this spicy garlic aioli and leftovers (which keep for up to ten days in the fridge) can be spread on sandwiches, served with any meat or fish, or even used as a dip with other veggies—although I doubt you'll have much left over, since it's so good.

---

*Serves 4 to 6*

—

¼ cup avocado oil

12 ounces shishito peppers

1 teaspoon flaky sea salt

Spicy Garlic Aioli
(recipe follows)

1. Heat the avocado oil in a large skillet over medium-high heat. Once the oil is hot, add the peppers. Cook, sautéing occasionally, until they've blistered, about 10 minutes. Transfer the peppers to a paper towel–lined plate to blot the excess oil.

2. Sprinkle with the flaky sea salt and serve with the Spicy Garlic Aioli as a dipping sauce.

*(recipe continues)*

# spicy garlic aioli

*Makes about 1 cup*

—

4 to 8 cloves Roasted Garlic (page 263), depending on how much garlic you like

2 egg yolks

1 teaspoon Dijon mustard

¼ teaspoon lemon juice

1 cup avocado oil

1 teaspoon champagne vinegar

1 teaspoon cayenne pepper

Salt and freshly ground black pepper

1. Smash the garlic on a cutting board with the top of a knife to create a garlic paste.

2. Place a dish towel on the countertop to prevent the bowl from moving. Place a large bowl on top of the towel. Combine the egg yolks, mustard, and lemon juice. Slowly drizzle in the avocado oil, whisking vigorously for 2 to 3 minutes, or until the mixture is completely combined and has thickened substantially. Add the vinegar, cayenne pepper, garlic, and salt and pepper to taste and whisk to combine. Let the Spicy Garlic Aioli sit in the fridge for 10 to 15 minutes for the flavors to combine.

# green chili chicken dip

Make this when you need to bring something to a friend's house—because it's a safe bet that most people will like it, it keeps well, and it just needs to be accompanied by some tortilla chips. I've also eaten leftovers cold, right out of the fridge . . . that's how good it is.

---

*Serves 4 to 6*

—

1 teaspoon extra-virgin olive oil

1 small yellow onion, chopped

6 scallions, white and green parts, chopped

4 cloves garlic, minced

2 Perfectly Cooked Chicken Thighs (page 248), shredded

¼ cup mayo

¼ cup sour cream

½ cup green enchilada sauce

1 (4-ounce) can diced green chiles, drained

¼ cup chopped fresh cilantro

1 teaspoon salt

½ teaspoon garlic powder

1 teaspoon chili powder

½ teaspoon smoked paprika

½ teaspoon onion powder

1 teaspoon ground cumin

1 jalapeño, seeds removed, finely chopped

¾ cup grated cheddar cheese

1 (32-ounce) bag tortilla chips, for serving

1. Preheat the oven to 350°F.

2. In a large skillet, warm the olive oil over medium heat. Add the onion, scallions, and garlic. Sauté until tender, about 5 minutes. Transfer the onion mixture to a large bowl.

3. Add the chicken, mayo, sour cream, enchilada sauce, chiles, cilantro, salt, garlic powder, chili powder, smoked paprika, onion powder, cumin, and jalapeño to the gooey onion dip mixture. Stir to combine.

4. Place the mixture in an 8 × 8-inch baking dish. Sprinkle the cheddar on top.

5. Bake, uncovered, for 20 to 23 minutes, or until bubbling. Serve warm with tortilla chips.

# dessert

# gluten-free maple date brownies

Some of my favorite memories with my mom are making brownies when I was in junior high. I also went on a crazy brownie kick in my early twenties, making them once a week. You can always count on brownies to put you in a good mood. These brownies are great because they're super moist and most of their sweetness comes from dates, which are full of vitamins, minerals, fiber, and antioxidants.

---

*Makes 9*

—

Virgin coconut oil, for the pan

6 large dates, pitted

1¼ cups cashew butter

¾ cup pure maple syrup

1 teaspoon pure vanilla extract

½ cup plus 1 tablespoon oat flour

⅓ cup raw cacao powder

2 teaspoons baking soda

2 teaspoons baking powder

Salt

1. Preheat the oven to 350°F. Line a 9 × 9-inch baking dish with parchment paper and lightly grease with coconut oil. Set aside.

2. Place the dates in a small saucepan over high heat and add enough water to cover them. Bring the water to a boil and let simmer for 2 minutes. Drain, and place the dates in the bowl of a food processor.

3. Add the cashew butter, maple syrup, and vanilla to the dates. Pulse until the date mixture is smooth and fully combined, about 30 seconds.

4. In a medium bowl, combine the flour, cacao powder, baking soda, baking powder, and a pinch of salt.

5. Add the date mixture to the flour mixture and mix well.

6. Pour the batter into the prepared baking dish. Smooth the top with a spatula (wet the spatula if needed to prevent sticking).

7. Bake for 28 to 30 minutes, until a toothpick comes out clean.

8. Let the brownies cool completely before cutting into squares.

# four-ingredient nut butter cookies

These cookies are awesome because you can use whatever nut butter you have in your pantry. And if you have nut allergies, they're also really good with SunButter. Not overly sweet, they're the perfect little afternoon pick-me-up. I consider these guys to be a healthy treat, since they're gluten- and dairy-free—so go ahead and have two.

*Makes 15 to 18*

—

1 cup nut butter, such as almond, cashew, or macadamia nut (or SunButter for a nut-free option)

1 cup coconut sugar

1 teaspoon pure vanilla extract

1 large egg

Flaky sea salt

1. Preheat the oven to 350°F. Line a large baking sheet with parchment paper.

2. In a large bowl, mix the nut butter, coconut sugar, vanilla, and egg together until combined.

3. Place 1 heaping tablespoon per cookie on the prepared baking sheet, leaving 1 inch between each. Sprinkle each cookie with a little flaky sea salt.

4. Bake, turning the baking sheet around halfway through, until golden brown, 10 to 15 minutes.

5. Let the cookies cool 10 minutes before eating.

6. The cookies will keep well in a zip-top bag on the counter for up to 7 days.

# skillet carrot cake
## with cream cheese frosting

Carrot cake is my all-time-favorite dessert. If you haven't had cream cheese frosting yet, then get ready because you're gonna want to put it on all your baked goods. And you most definitely can. A lot of carrot cake recipes have raisins in them, but I left them out in this one. I think they distract from the simplicity of the cake.

---

*Serves 6 to 8*

—

½ cup virgin coconut oil, melted, plus more for the pan

1 cup all-purpose flour

½ cup almond flour

½ cup coconut sugar

2 teaspoons baking soda

1 teaspoon baking powder

½ teaspoon salt

1 teaspoon ground cinnamon

¼ teaspoon ground nutmeg

¼ teaspoon ground cloves

¼ teaspoon cardamom

2 large eggs

1 cup plain yogurt

2 teaspoons pure vanilla extract

1 cup finely grated carrots (about 2 medium carrots)

½ cup unsweetened shredded coconut

1 cup Cream Cheese Frosting (page 265)

1. Preheat the oven to 350°F. Grease a 10-inch ovenproof skillet with coconut oil and set aside.

2. In a large bowl, combine both flours, the coconut sugar, baking soda, baking powder, salt, cinnamon, nutmeg, cloves, and cardamom.

3. In a medium bowl, whisk together the eggs, coconut oil, yogurt, and vanilla. Add the wet ingredients to the dry ingredients and fold to combine. Add the carrots and coconut and fold again until just combined.

4. Pour the batter into the prepared skillet. Smooth the top with a spatula.

5. Bake for 28 to 32 minutes, until a toothpick comes out clean in the center and the top is golden brown. Cool the cake completely before frosting.

# dark chocolate
# nut butter buckeyes

I could eat one thousand buckeyes, they're just so easy to keep popping in your mouth. And they aren't crazy sweet, so you can actually get away with eating a bunch without getting a stomachache. I like having these on hand for the times that I just want a little something after dinner. "Buckeyes" got their name because they resemble the poisonous nut of the Ohio buckeye, the state tree of Ohio.

*Makes 10 to 12*

—

¼ cup creamy almond butter

¼ cup cashew butter

3 tablespoons pure maple syrup

¼ cup plus 1 tablespoon coconut flour

1 teaspoon pure vanilla extract

Salt

—

### chocolate coating

¼ cup virgin coconut oil

¼ cup raw cacao powder

2 tablespoons pure maple syrup

½ teaspoon pure vanilla extract

1. Line a large baking sheet with parchment paper and set aside.

2. In a large bowl, combine both nut butters, the maple syrup, coconut flour, vanilla, and a pinch of salt. Roll the mixture into golf ball–size balls and place them on the prepared baking sheet. Place the baking sheet in the freezer for 10 minutes, until hardened.

3. Meanwhile, make the chocolate coating: In a small saucepan over medium heat, melt the coconut oil. Whisk in the cacao powder, maple syrup, and vanilla until combined and smooth. Remove the saucepan from the heat and allow the chocolate to cool until almost at room temperature.

4. Take the balls out of the freezer. Roll a ball between your hands for a second, then place a toothpick in the center. Holding the toothpick, dip the ball in the chocolate, covering all of it except the top around the hole the toothpick has made. Place the chocolate-coated ball back on the baking sheet, without the toothpick. Repeat with the remaining balls.

5. Place the chocolate-coated balls back in the freezer for 15 minutes, until the chocolate has hardened. The buckeyes will keep well in the fridge for up to 10 days.

# banana pudding
## with homemade vanilla wafers

This banana pudding is for my sweet Jax, because he loves anything banana. And when I first made these wafers, the kids kept going on and on about how good they were. The wafer recipe makes a ton but we always power through them quickly (I guess that's what happens when there are three kids). I actually think this is one of my kids' favorites in the whole book. The layers of banana pudding, chopped wafers, and sliced bananas make for a fun presentation. If the kids are having friends over for dinner, I'll make this for dessert.

*Serves 6*

—

2 large ripe bananas, plus
1 to 2 ripe bananas (optional),
sliced, for serving

½ cup raw cane sugar

2 tablespoons arrowroot
powder

¼ teaspoon salt

1 (13.5-ounce) can full-fat
coconut milk

¼ teaspoon fresh lemon juice

4 large egg yolks

½ teaspoon pure vanilla
extract

2 tablespoons virgin
coconut oil

6 to 12 Vanilla Wafers
(recipe follows)

1. Place 2 bananas in a food processor and pulse until completely smooth.

2. In a medium saucepan over medium heat, whisk together the sugar, arrowroot powder, salt, and coconut milk and bring to a simmer. Add the bananas and lemon juice and whisk to combine.

3. Place the egg yolks in a small bowl. Give them a little whisk, then add to the banana mixture. Bring the banana mixture to a boil, then simmer, whisking occasionally, for 10 to 15 minutes, until thickened. Remove the saucepan from the heat. Stir in the vanilla and coconut oil.

4. Pour the pudding into a large bowl and place plastic wrap on top. Place in the fridge to cool completely, about 2 hours.

5. To serve, chop the wafers and sprinkle on top of the pudding. Or create layers by placing some pudding on the bottom of a mason jar or large glass, followed by chopped wafers, sliced bananas, more pudding, more sliced bananas, and topped with more chopped wafers.

*(recipe continues)*

# vanilla wafers

*Makes 15 to 20*

—

½ cup (1 stick) unsalted butter, at room temperature

1⅔ cups powdered sugar

3 large egg whites, at room temperature

1 large egg, at room temperature

1⅓ cups all-purpose flour

2 teaspoons pure vanilla extract

¼ teaspoon salt

1. Preheat the oven to 350°F. Line a large baking sheet with parchment paper.

2. Place the butter and sugar in the bowl of a stand mixer, then beat high until light and fluffy, about 3 minutes. Slowly add the egg whites and mix until combined. Add the whole egg and mix well. Add the flour, vanilla, and salt and mix until just combined. The batter will be wet.

3. Place the batter into a piping bag or a large zip-top bag with the corner cut off. Pipe the batter onto the prepared baking sheet, about 2 teaspoons per wafer, leaving about 1 inch between each wafer.

4. Bake for 18 to 20 minutes, until golden brown.

5. Let the wafers cool for 5 minutes before eating. The wafers will keep well in an airtight container on the counter for up to 10 days, if you can get them to last that long. You can also freeze them for up to 6 months.

# edible peanut butter chocolate chip cookie dough

I made this cookie dough with my oldest, Cam, in mind. He loves all things peanut butter, and it's safe to say my whole family loves cookie dough. That was always my favorite part about making cookies as a kid, licking the bowl, so I understand why my kids love it, too. This recipe is gluten- and dairy-free, so there's no need to stress if you accidentally eat the whole thing.

---

*Makes 3 to 4 cups*

—

1 cup pure maple syrup

¾ cup smooth peanut butter

⅓ cup virgin coconut oil, melted

3 cups almond flour

2 teaspoons pure vanilla extract

Salt

1 cup semisweet chocolate chips

1. In a large bowl, combine the maple syrup, peanut butter, coconut oil, flour, vanilla, and a pinch of salt. Fold in the chocolate chips.

2. Eat right away with a spoon!

3. The cookie dough will keep well in an airtight container in the fridge for up to 7 days.

# gluten-free lemon strawberry blondies

I'm a lemon fanatic so I go crazy for these blondies. They're light, making them perfect after a big meal or as a little snack. The cooked strawberries give big bursts of sweetness in each bite. If I'm being honest, I've actually even had these for breakfast with coffee. Yeah, I said it.

---

*Makes 16*

—

1½ cups oat flour

½ teaspoon baking powder

¼ teaspoon salt

⅓ cup (almost ¾ stick) unsalted butter, at room temperature

½ cup raw cane sugar

1 large egg

1 teaspoon pure vanilla extract

¼ cup fresh lemon juice (from about 2 lemons)

1 cup chopped strawberries

1. Preheat the oven to 350°F. Line an 8 × 5-inch baking dish with parchment paper.

2. In a large bowl, combine the oat flour, baking powder, and a pinch of salt.

3. Place the butter, sugar, egg, and vanilla in the bowl of a stand mixer, then beat on high until light and slightly fluffy, about 1 minute. Add the lemon juice and mix well. While the blade is running, slowly add the flour mixture and beat until combined, about 30 seconds.

4. Fold in the strawberries. Pour the batter into the prepared baking dish, using a spatula to smooth the top.

5. Bake for 25 to 30 minutes, until a toothpick comes out clean and the edges are slightly golden brown.

6. Let the blondies cool for 10 minutes in the pan. Using the parchment paper, lift the blondies from the pan and place on a cooling rack to cool for another 10 minutes before cutting into squares.

# blueberry and blackberry skillet cobbler

Cobbler recipes are relatively easy (well, this one is) and they're relatively healthy, but they still check that sweet-craving box. I love this on a warm summer night when I'm sitting outside with friends watching the kiddos play. One major disclaimer: It's been known to make your teeth a little blue! The color goes away, though—I promise. Just maybe don't make this for a first date.

---

*Serves 6 to 8*

—

Virgin coconut oil, for the pan

2 cups blueberries

2 cups blackberries, coarsely chopped

1 teaspoon fresh lemon juice

1 teaspoon pure vanilla extract

¼ cup coconut sugar

—

**topping**

1 cup gluten-free rolled oats

½ cup almond flour

1 tablespoon ground flaxseed

½ teaspoon ground cinnamon

1 teaspoon pure vanilla extract

¼ cup virgin coconut oil, melted

3 tablespoons coconut sugar

Salt

Vanilla ice cream, for serving (optional)

1. Preheat the oven to 350°F. Lightly grease a 10-inch cast-iron skillet or other ovenproof skillet with coconut oil.

2. In a large bowl, combine both berries, the lemon juice, vanilla, and coconut sugar. Place the berry mixture in the skillet.

3. Make the topping: In another large bowl, combine the oats, flour, flaxseed, cinnamon, vanilla, coconut oil, coconut sugar, and a pinch of salt. Sprinkle the oat mixture on top of the berries, covering them completely.

4. Bake for 30 to 35 minutes, until the berries are bubbling and the oats are golden brown.

5. Let the cobbler cool for 10 minutes before serving.

6. To serve, eat as is or, if desired, put a scoop of vanilla ice cream on top.

# gluten-free cold brew brownie cookies

Gooey and delicious, these brownie cookies are the perfect boost when you want something chocolaty with a caffeine kick. I love coffee-flavored everything, so I had to include it in a recipe, and I thought what better way than with chocolate (mochas, anyone?).

*Makes 20*

—

½ cup (1 stick) unsalted butter, at room temperature

1 cup coconut sugar

2 large eggs

4 ounces cold-brewed coffee

1 teaspoon pure vanilla extract

¾ cup raw cacao powder

¼ teaspoon arrowroot powder

½ teaspoon baking powder

1 cup plus 2 tablespoons all-purpose gluten-free flour

¼ teaspoon salt

1. Preheat the oven to 350°F. Line a large baking sheet with parchment paper.

2. Place the butter and coconut sugar in the bowl of a stand mixer, then beat on high until a little fluffy, about 2 minutes. While the blade is running, add the eggs, one at a time, and mix until combined. Add the coffee and vanilla and mix. Add the cacao powder, arrowroot powder, baking powder, flour, and salt. Mix until everything is combined.

3. Using a wet spoon, scoop tablespoon-size balls onto the prepared baking sheet. Flatten each cookie with the back of the spoon until it's about ½ inch thick.

4. Bake for 12 to 14 minutes, until cooked through.

5. Let the cookies cool for 10 minutes before enjoying.

# gluten-free lemon pound cake

I could eat this light and lemony cake any time of the day. The homemade cream cheese frosting takes it to the next level, but you can also use your favorite store-bought frosting to save time. I usually make this cake for the Fourth of July, but I leave out the lemon juice and lemon zest, and I top it with sliced strawberries and whole blueberries to make the design of the American flag. I've been making that cake since I was little, and now I make it every single year with my children.

*Serves 12 to 16*

—

Virgin coconut oil, for the pan

4 large eggs

⅔ cup pure maple syrup

⅔ cup (almost 1½ sticks) unsalted butter, at room temperature

½ cup plus 3 tablespoons almond milk

2 teaspoons pure vanilla extract

3 tablespoons fresh lemon juice (from about 1½ lemons)

1 teaspoon lemon zest

2 cups almond flour

½ cup coconut flour

1 teaspoon baking soda

¼ teaspoon salt

1 cup Cream Cheese Frosting (page 265)

1. Preheat the oven to 350°F. Lightly grease a 9 × 9-inch baking dish with coconut oil.

2. Place the eggs in the bowl of a stand mixer, then beat on high until frothy, about 30 seconds. Add the maple syrup, butter, almond milk, vanilla, lemon juice, and lemon zest and beat until combined, another few seconds. Add the almond flour, coconut flour, baking soda, and salt and mix until just combined, about 10 seconds, being careful not to overmix.

3. Pour the batter into the prepared baking dish and bake for 35 to 40 minutes, until a toothpick comes out clean.

4. Cool the cake completely before frosting.

5. The pound cake will keep well in an airtight container on the counter for up to 5 days.

# individual dairy-free key lime pies

My kids think these mini key lime pies are fun because you can eat them like cupcakes. I like them because, as a key lime pie obsessive, I have automatic portion control. These need an hour in the freezer to chill, so be sure to make them ahead of when you want to eat them.

---

*Makes 12*

—

### filling

1½ cups raw cashews

½ cup fresh key lime juice (from 4 to 6 limes)

1 tablespoon lime zest

1¼ cups full-fat coconut milk

⅓ cup pure maple syrup

—

### crust

7 ounces graham crackers

¾ cup cashew butter

Salt

Lime zest, for garnish

1. Preheat the oven to 375°F. Prepare a muffin tin with liners.

2. Place the cashews in a small bowl and cover with hot water. Let sit for 15 minutes, then drain.

3. Make the crust: In the bowl of a food processor, pulse the graham crackers until they're fine crumbs, about 30 seconds. Add the cashew butter and a pinch of salt and pulse until a loosely formed, sticky, clumpy dough is formed, another 30 seconds or so.

4. Spoon the graham cracker mixture into the lined cups of the muffin tin, pressing firmly on the bottom and up the sides, until each is almost to the top.

5. Bake for 10 to 12 minutes, or until golden brown. Let cool for 15 minutes.

6. Meanwhile make the filling: Place the cashews, lime juice, lime zest, coconut milk, and maple syrup in a high-powered blender and blend on high until smooth, 30 to 45 seconds.

7. Pour the lime mixture into the cups of the muffin tin, until each is full. Freeze for 1 hour to harden.

8. To serve, garnish each key lime pie with a sprinkle of lime zest. The pies will keep well in the fridge for up to 7 days.

# gluten- and dairy-free
# chocolate chip pistachio cookies

I wanted to change up the classic chocolate chip cookie by giving them an extra little crunch. Enter pistachios. I've been on a pistachio kick lately, even making Pistachio Milk (page 261), so throwing them into a chocolate chip recipe was a no-brainer. The first few times I made these, I actually used butter, but believe it or not, I think they're better *without* it (they don't get as fluffy with butter). I always throw half of the baked cookies in a zip-top bag into the freezer (they'll last up to 6 months), and I actually love eating a cookie right out of the freezer . . . Am I the only one?!

---

*Makes 18*

—

2 cups almond flour

½ teaspoon baking soda

½ teaspoon salt

1 large egg

1 teaspoon pure vanilla extract

¼ cup virgin coconut oil, melted

½ cup pure maple syrup

½ cup semisweet chocolate chips

½ cup chopped pistachios

1. Preheat the oven to 350°F. Line a large baking sheet with parchment paper.

2. In a large bowl, combine the flour, baking soda, and salt.

3. In a medium bowl, whisk together the egg, vanilla, coconut oil, and maple syrup. Pour the wet ingredients into the dry ingredients and mix well. Fold in the chocolate chips and pistachios.

4. Spoon the dough onto the baking sheet, about 1½ tablespoons per cookie, leaving a little space between each one.

5. Bake for 12 to 15 minutes, until golden brown.

6. Let the cookies cool for 10 minutes before eating. The cookies will keep well in an airtight container on the counter for up to 5 days or in the freezer for up to 6 months.

# n'ice cream three ways

I first discovered how great frozen bananas can be in my early twenties. I would freeze them to throw into my smoothies and, let me tell you, once you put a frozen banana into a smoothie, you'll never go back to a regular one. They make smoothies so incredibly creamy. That's also when I discovered "n'ice cream" (creamy, thick, banana "ice cream"). If you have frozen bananas on hand, like I always do, this can be made in two minutes.

---

*Makes about 2 cups*

—

**vanilla n'ice cream**

3 small bananas, frozen

½ cup almond milk

1 teaspoon pure vanilla extract

Pinch of salt

—

**chocolate n'ice cream**

3 small bananas, frozen

½ cup almond milk

1 teaspoon pure vanilla extract

Pinch of salt

2 teaspoons raw cacao powder

—

**strawberry n'ice cream**

3 small bananas, frozen

½ cup almond milk

1 teaspoon pure vanilla extract

Pinch of salt

¾ cup coarsely chopped strawberries

1. Place the bananas, almond milk, vanilla, salt, and (if you're making chocolate or strawberry) any additional ingredients in a high-powered blender and blend on high until smooth, about 45 seconds. You might have to blend for a few seconds, then push the mixture down with a spoon before continuing to mix.

2. Eat right away. The leftover n'ice cream will store well in the freezer for up to a month.

# oatmeal cream pies

I was already finished writing this cookbook when Jaxon came home with the packaged oatmeal cream pies from school. I read the ingredients and begged him not to eat them. So, I came up with this recipe for my little man.

---

*Makes 13 large pies*

—

1 cup (2 sticks) unsalted butter, at room temperature

¾ cup coconut sugar

½ cup raw cane sugar

2 large eggs

1 teaspoon pure vanilla extract

1½ cups oat flour

1 teaspoon baking soda

1 teaspoon ground cinnamon

½ teaspoon salt

3 cups gluten-free rolled oats

—

**filling**

¾ cup (1½ sticks) unsalted butter, at room temperature

2½ cups powdered sugar

1 teaspoon pure vanilla extract

1 tablespoon full-fat coconut milk

1. Preheat the oven to 350°F. Line a large baking sheet with parchment paper.

2. Place the butter and both sugars in the bowl of a stand mixer, then beat on high until light and fluffy, about 3 minutes. Add the eggs and vanilla and mix.

3. In a medium bowl, whisk together the flour, baking soda, cinnamon, and salt. While the blade is running, slowly add the flour mixture to the butter mixture until just combined. Fold in the oats.

4. Spoon about 2 tablespoons of the dough per cookie onto the prepared baking sheet, leaving a little room in between each one. Bake for 10 to 15 minutes, until golden brown. Cool completely before making the pies.

5. Meanwhile, make the filling: Place the butter in the bowl of a stand mixer, then beat on high until light and fluffy, about 5 minutes. While the blade is running on low, slowly add the powdered sugar and mix until combined. Add the vanilla and coconut milk and beat on medium speed for 3 to 5 minutes, until combined and fluffy.

6. Spread some filling, about 1 tablespoon, on a cookie, or place the filling in a piping bag and pipe onto a cookie. Place another cookie on top and give it a little squeeze to keep them together. Repeat with the remaining cookies.

7. The cream pies will keep well in an airtight container on the counter for up to 5 days or in the fridge for up to 7 days.

# staples

# chicken thighs
# two ways

The key to getting really moist chicken is to not overcook it. For skin-on chicken thighs, I like getting the skin really crispy (that's actually my favorite part). You could even just make this chicken as a main dish. When the chicken is cooked perfectly, that's all you need—because it will be juicy and flavorful. This recipe is for both bone-in, skin-on chicken thighs *and* boneless, skinless chicken thighs.

---

## perfectly cooked chicken thighs

*Makes 4 thighs*

—

4 large boneless, skinless chicken thighs (about 1 pound)

2 tablespoons extra-virgin olive oil

1 teaspoon salt

¼ teaspoon freshly ground black pepper

1. Preheat the oven to 375°F. Line a medium baking dish with parchment paper.

2. Place the chicken in the prepared baking dish. Pour the olive oil on top of the chicken and season with salt and pepper. Use your hands to coat the chicken.

3. Roast the chicken for 20 to 24 minutes, until it is cooked through and the internal temperature reaches 165°F.

4. Let the chicken rest for 5 minutes.

5. The chicken thighs will keep well in the fridge for up to 5 days.

# bone-in, skin-on chicken thighs

*Makes 4 thighs*

—

4 large bone-in, skin-on chicken thighs (about 1 pound)

2 tablespoons extra-virgin olive oil

1 teaspoon salt

¼ teaspoon freshly ground black pepper

1. Preheat the oven to 375°F. Line a large baking dish with parchment paper.

2. Place the chicken in the prepared baking dish, skin-side up. Coat the chicken with the olive oil and season with the salt and pepper, making sure to get some under the skin.

3. Roast the chicken for 25 to 28 minutes, until it is cooked through. Turn the oven to broil and roast for 4 to 7 minutes, until the skin is crispy and golden brown.

4. Let the chicken rest for 5 minutes.

5. The chicken thighs will keep well in the fridge for up to 5 days.

# tzatziki sauce

This light and fresh yogurt dip is perfect with so many dishes. It goes great with Mediterranean Meatballs (page 169) and Grilled Lamb Skewers (page 139) or make it as a dip to accompany the Gluten-Free Naan (see page 207). I also like throwing tzatziki sauce in salads, if I have extra on hand.

---

*Makes 1¼ cups*

—

2 Persian cucumbers, grated (about 1 cup)

1½ tablespoons fresh lemon juice

1 clove garlic, minced

1 cup plain yogurt

1½ teaspoons white wine vinegar

1 tablespoon chopped fresh dill

¼ teaspoon salt

Extra-virgin olive oil, for drizzling

1. Place the grated cucumbers in a dish towel or nut milk bag and squeeze out the extra moisture over the sink. Transfer to a medium bowl.

2. Add the lemon juice, garlic, yogurt, vinegar, dill, and salt and mix well.

3. To serve, drizzle a little olive oil over the top.

4. The sauce will keep well in an airtight container in the fridge for up to 7 days.

# chili oil

I always have this oil on hand, as it's great in my Citrus Salmon
(page 151) and Turmeric Fried Eggs with Crispy Kale (page 59). I'll also
drizzle some on scrambled eggs, different meat, you name it. The oil
will harden in the fridge, so take it out five to ten minutes before you
want to use it or, if you're in a time pinch, you could run the jar under
hot water.

---

*Makes about 1 cup*

—

1 cup avocado oil

2 tablespoons red pepper
flakes

2 cloves garlic, crushed

1 small shallot, peeled
and halved

Salt

1. In a small saucepan over low heat, mix the avocado oil,
red pepper flakes, garlic, shallot, and a pinch of salt. Cook
for 10 minutes to allow the flavors to combine, stirring
occasionally.

2. Strain, then place the oil in a mason jar or other airtight
container.

3. The oil will keep well in the fridge for up to 1 month.

# pesto

I live for pesto. I throw it on eggs in the morning and pasta in the evening, eat it with meat, have been known to dip veggies in it, and could totally eat it straight off a spoon—nothing is off-limits. I stand by the thought that pesto is always better fresh and homemade, and since it's not too complicated, this is well worth the effort.

---

*Makes about ¾ cup*

—

2 cups packed fresh
basil leaves

3 tablespoons pine nuts

2 small cloves garlic, coarsely
chopped

1½ tablespoons fresh
lemon juice

¼ cup grated Manchego or
Parmesan cheese

Salt and freshly ground
black pepper

¼ cup extra-virgin olive oil

1. In a food processor, combine the basil, pine nuts, garlic, lemon juice, Manchego, a big pinch of salt, and pepper until smooth. Slowly drizzle in the olive oil while the blade is still running, until combined. Season again with salt and pepper to taste.

2. The pesto will keep well in an airtight container in the fridge for up to 14 days.

# warm berry sauce

Okay, full disclosure: This recipe is a repeat from my cookbook *True Comfort*, but it's so dang good, and it goes perfectly with so many dishes, that I just had to include it here, too. It's thick and sweet, and you can add it to yogurt parfaits (see page 38) and crepes (see page 44). You could also put it on vanilla ice cream. Yum.

---

*Makes about ½ cup*

—

1 tablespoon arrowroot powder

1 teaspoon fresh lemon juice

½ cup fresh blueberries, blackberries, raspberries, or strawberries (if using strawberries, chop them into smaller pieces)

3 tablespoons pure maple syrup

1. In a small bowl, mix the arrowroot powder with 1 tablespoon water and whisk to combine.

2. In a small saucepan over medium-high heat, combine the lemon juice, berries, maple syrup, and 3 more tablespoons water. Bring the mixture to a boil, then reduce to a simmer and cook for 4 minutes, until the berries are tender. Add the dissolved arrowroot and cook for about 5 minutes, until the sauce has thickened substantially.

3. The sauce will keep well in an airtight container in the fridge for up to 10 days.

# seaweed crumble

I started making this to throw on all of our sushi bowls, but now the kids will eat it just as a snack as well. It's salty and sweet and takes two minutes to throw together. I'll enlist the kids to tear the seaweed because they think it's fun, and I love having them in the kitchen with me.

---

*Makes about ½ cup*

—

2 nori sheets

1 teaspoon coconut sugar

2 teaspoons toasted sesame oil

1 tablespoon toasted sesame seeds

Salt

1. In a large bowl, using your hands, crumble and rip the seaweed sheets until they are in tiny pieces. Add the coconut sugar, sesame oil, sesame seeds, and a pinch of salt and mix with your hands until combined.

2. The leftovers will keep well in an airtight container on the counter for up to 10 days.

# cauliflower rice

Cauliflower rice is one of my favorite kitchen hacks because you can do so many things with it. I use it to make pizza crust and Cauliflower Oatmeal (page 60), and I swap regular rice for cauliflower rice in all of my bowls whenever I'm trying to be extra healthy (that's usually when I'm two weeks out from a photo shoot). It has a mild flavor, which allows it to take on whatever flavors you want.

---

*Makes about 2 cups*

—

1 medium head cauliflower, cut into small pieces

1. In a food processor, pulse the cauliflower until it resembles pieces of rice, 15 to 30 seconds. Depending on how big the food processor is, you might need to do this in batches. Transfer the mixture to a large zip-top bag.

2. The rice will keep well in an airtight container in the fridge for up to 7 days.

# nut milk three ways

I always have some sort of nut milk in my fridge. Since I use nut milk so often, I try to switch it up for different flavors. I did a food allergy test a year ago, and almonds were my number one allergen, probably because I was having an almond milk latte every morning in addition to almond milk in smoothies, so I had to eliminate almonds for six months. During that time, I started making Brazil nut milk, pistachio nut milk, and macadamia nut milk regularly, and I fell in love with all three. Brazil nut milk is great for baking and cooking because the flavor is so mild. Since they're richer, I prefer pistachio milk and macadamia nut milk for lattes and smoothies. If I know I'll be using my nut milk for cooking or smoothies, I leave it plain (no maple syrup or vanilla), but if I'll be using it for lattes or hot chocolate for the kids, then I sweeten it or add some flavor.

---

*Makes about 4 cups*

—

**Brazil nut milk, pistachio milk, or macadamia nut milk**

1 cup whole, raw Brazil nuts, pistachios, or macadamia nuts

4 cups filtered water

1 to 2 tablespoons pure maple syrup (optional)

½ teaspoon pure vanilla extract (optional)

1. Place the nuts in a medium bowl. Completely cover the nuts with hot water and soak for 8 hours, or up to overnight, then drain and rinse.

2. Place the nuts in a high-powered blender with the filtered water. Blend on high until smooth, about 1 minute. Using a cheesecloth or a nut milk bag, strain the nut milk into a large bowl. Discard any pulp or keep to use for another recipe of your liking.

3. If using sweetener or flavor, place the milk back in the blender after a quick rinse to remove any leftover pulp and add the maple syrup and vanilla. Blend until combined, about 30 seconds.

4. The milk will keep well in a glass container in the fridge for up to 7 days.

# spicy mayo

This probably didn't need to be an actual recipe, but I included it in this book because I use spicy mayo on so many dishes, like the Salmon Bowl (page 95). When it comes to mayo, I always make sure I get one made with avocado oil, as it won't create inflammation in the body like the canola oil and soybean oil you find in a lot of mainstream mayos.

*Makes about ½ cup*

—

½ cup mayo

¼ cup Sriracha

1. In a small bowl, whisk together the mayo and Sriracha until combined.

2. The mayo will keep well in the fridge for up to 14 days.

# roasted garlic

*Makes 1 head garlic*

—

1 head garlic

Extra-virgin olive oil

Coarse sea salt

1. Preheat the oven to 400°F.

2. Cut the top off the head of garlic and peel away the outer layer. Drizzle the head with olive oil and sprinkle with one big pinch of salt. Wrap the garlic in foil, leaving a small hole so heat can escape. Bake for 35 minutes.

3. Let cool slightly, then squeeze out the garlic and mash it, or keep it whole. The garlic keeps well in olive oil for up to a week in the fridge.

# ranch dressing

This has been a staple in my house for years. Yes, my kids love ranch dressing (it's the only way my boys will eat salad), but I find uses for it, too. I drizzle it on Buffalo Chicken Pizza (page 166) and BBQ Chicken Pizza (page 167) and use it as a veggie dip. I've changed this recipe over the years from using vegan mayo (I used to like it for its bland flavor) to using an avocado-based mayo now (I like the Primal Kitchen brand), but feel free to use your fave.

---

*Makes about 1½ cups*

—

1½ cups mayo

¼ cup almond milk or Brazil Nut Milk (page 261)

1 tablespoon apple cider vinegar

1 tablespoon chopped fresh parsley

1½ teaspoons onion powder

1 teaspoon garlic powder

1 teaspoon dill

¼ teaspoon freshly ground black pepper

1. Place the mayo, almond milk, vinegar, parsley, onion powder, garlic powder, dill, and black pepper in a high-powered blender. Blend until combined and creamy.

2. The dressing will keep well in an airtight container in the fridge for up to 10 days.

# cream cheese frosting

It doesn't get much better than cream cheese frosting. It's made from two of the most delicious ingredients on the planet: cream cheese and sugar. And it's my weakness! This frosting is perfection on the Skillet Carrot Cake (page 224), but you can really use it to top any cake or cupcake. It's also great on cookies. Pretty much any dessert is a safe bet.

---

*Makes 1 cup*

—

¼ cup (½ stick) unsalted butter, at room temperature

4 ounces cream cheese, at room temperature

2 teaspoons pure vanilla extract

1½ cups powdered sugar

1. Place the butter and cream cheese in the bowl of a stand mixer, then beat on high until fluffy, about 3 minutes. Add the vanilla and mix until combined. While the blade is running on low, slowly add the powdered sugar until combined, about 1 minute.

2. The frosting will keep well in an airtight container in the fridge for up to 7 days.

# acknowledgments

I loved every second of creating this cookbook, and I can easily say this book is the one I'm most proud of. This book never would have happened if my editor, Dervla Kelly, didn't encourage me to do this one on my own. So, Dervla, thank you for believing in me from the very beginning of my journey as an author and for continuing to believe in me all these years later.

Thank you to everyone at the Rodale team for bringing this cookbook to life: Katherine Leak, Patricia Shaw, Mia Johnson, and Stephanie Huntwork. Aubrie, Glenn, and Fanny, thank you for making my recipes look way better than I ever could.

Thank you, glam squad—Robert, Marwa, and Dani—for all the laughs and for making *me* look better than I ever could. Susan and Jack, thank you for your continued support and hard work with all you do.

A massive thank-you to my kids for eating the same meals over and over, for giving me their honest opinions, for grounding me, and for inspiring me every single day.

And last but not least, to everyone who has supported me over the years . . . I know how lucky I am to do what I do, and it's because of you all, so thank you!

# index

Note: Page references in *italics* indicate photographs.

also by kristin cavallari
*True Comfort*
*True Roots*
*Balancing in Heels*

Text copyright © 2023 by Kristin Cavallari
Photographs copyright © 2023
by Aubrie Pick

All rights reserved.
Published in the United States by
Rodale Books, an imprint of
Random House, a division of
Penguin Random House LLC, New York.
RodaleBooks.com
RandomHouseBooks.com

RODALE and the Plant colophon are
registered trademarks of Penguin
Random House LLC.

Library of Congress Cataloging-in-
Publication Data is available upon
request

ISBN 978-0-593-57878-0
Ebook ISBN 978-0-593-57879-7

Printed in China

Interior and cover design by Mia Johnson
Cover photographs by Aubrey Pick

10 9 8 7 6 5 4 3 2 1

First Edition